MESSAGES

A Survivor's Letter to a Young German

EUGENE HEIMLER

A New Philosophy of Life and Living After the Holocaust

INTRODUCTION

Eugene Heimler, in his captivatingly poetic style, takes you with him on a life-transforming journey through seas of imagination and rivers of tears; from storms of pain to pools of individual and communal wisdom as well as deep inside his self and yours.

His universal and autobiographical stories, like the vivid colors on the canvas of a water-color artist, flow and dynamically blend time dimensions into an expanding, cohesive whole.

The diversity of genre, time and metaphor is startling and reveals multiple layers of our physical, emotional and spiritual reality.

The author transcends time as he interweaves past, present and future into a tapestry of deep meaning and passion, stained by blood and marked by tears and joy.

This book is about the author's journey of losing, searching and re-finding his own identity and place in his physical, emotional and spiritual worlds. In his 'stream of consciousness' musings Heimler crosses time from biblical through medieval to modern human experiences of transformation through pain to self-discovery.

This artful intimate intertwining of personal, particular and universal themes draws the reader into Heimler's awe-inspiring multi-layered world of courageous introspection.

Messages illuminates how Heimler, as a Holocaust survivor, struggles to re-discover meaning, purpose and passion from his once shattered world. Working through these challenges leads him to existential questions about the very meaning of life:

What are the connections between life and what we call death?

How can meaning transcend suffering?

How can we find peace if we deny our worst hours?

How can we understand all the hatred that surrounds us?

How can hate be turned into creativity instead of self-destructiveness?

What can keep our love and our ability to love alive in the midst of atrocities or indifference?

Come, join this remarkable man in his quest for eternal wisdom!

Miriam Bracha Heimler

MESSAGE FROM THE HOLOCAUST:
"The Love of Man is the Love of God"

PART ONE

A SURVIVOR'S LETTER TO A YOUNG GERMAN

Dear young friend:

I keep meeting you all the time: in Berlin, in Frankfurt, in Hanover, in Munich and many other places in West Germany. Whenever we meet, there seems to be some kind of wall between us. I feel that you look at me as if I had come from another world, another planet. Emotionally there is sometimes strangeness between us. This strangeness can be broken; more often than not we break it, you and I.

The sense of strangeness is on both sides. On yours, because you know what has happened to me. The terms "concentration camp" and "holocaust" fill you with uneasiness, because you are the descendant of those who created them.

So the man who now stands before you becomes a symbol. You approach the symbol and begin to peel off the mask and slowly you begin to see the man. He is no different from you really, except older. His hair is turning white, yet his heart throbs with the same rhythm as yours.

On my part, I always remember. I remember a train journey just over twenty years ago from Paris to Milan, when I shared a compartment with a young German. He had not been a part of all the terrible things that had happened to me, to us. He could not have been a part; he was too young. His was a somewhat newer generation than mine. Yet somehow I could not make any contact with him.

That was a long time ago. I realized then that it would be a great triumph in my life if I could reach out to this young German. One day, I hoped, perhaps I would be able to do that. I wrote about this in my book called *"A Link in the Chain"*.

You see, today I can reach out to you. Let me tell you why.

In my work I keep hearing your voice. By the nature of my work, I have personal interviews with you. I listen to your life, achievements, problems, frustrations, anxieties, hopes and pleasures. And as I listen, I detect a tone that is so well known to me. I see my own life in all the things that you are concerned with.

When I see you face to face, person to person, eventually the wall – on my part – falls down. I see myself in you, as you perhaps see yourself in me. That is what human communication is all about.

But it is more than that.

You hold an image, and with that image goes fear. It is difficult to ask a father, an uncle, a mother, what really happened. Even if answers are forthcoming, they are evasive and shrouded in mystery. Your parents would say, *'they had to do what they had to do.'* Maybe … but surely there must be limits even to what is done out of duty.

They cannot answer you. They cannot tell you what really went on, what really happened. Some of them are deeply ashamed. Others still think they were right and hope that you and your friends and your children will one day revive the old ghost again.

They cannot speak. I can speak because I am a survivor.

And I want to speak to you so that the wall between us might vanish for good.

There will be things I shall tell you which will hurt you. That, believe me, is not my intention. But you have to know: not only in your head but also in your heart.

You have to know for your own sake so that no secrecy is left and so that, once the ghosts disappear, you see the truth in daylight.

You have to know for your children's sake too, who one day will also want to know.

But what I am talking about is more than mere knowledge of the past. I am talking about the world we live in now; - a world which is becoming ever more violent, dangerous, aggressive, insensitive to other people's needs, and cruel beyond words. A world in which people are dying because they are hungry, or because of their race, color or religion, or because wars and revolutions still destroy them. They are people like you and me, and they are still oppressed.

I have a dream, that one day I might tell you that all this can be changed. But first knowledge must come. And then, after knowledge, there must come a new philosophy about life and living. I believe that Judaism understood this philosophy about life and survival. So I shall tell you about this as well.

You see, I am a solitary man because I cannot follow movements, organizations, political parties, however fashionable they may be. I am suspicious because masses can be wrong too. Individuals can also be wrong if they give up their own individuality.

So what you will hear from me may not be popular at present, when mass movements are so powerful and the individual seems so unimportant.

Some slogans and trends sound revolutionary and modern and personal, yet I beg you to listen; because, if you listen carefully to what I want to say to you, you may find that the greatest revolution is the revolution and liberation of the mind and the soul.

I want to speak of these things for my own sake too. It is important for me to get it out of my system. And somehow as I speak I almost feel as though I were speaking perhaps on behalf of those who died in the camps.

I know one thing: Your generation must be given absolution. Blame and self-blame must be abandoned once and for all. <u>Because *you* are not guilty. Whatever your parents may have done or not done, *you* are not guilty!</u>

Those who died would never blame you. Anyone who holds you responsible for what you are not accountable for is guilty of being a Nazi, at least in his heart.

The unwillingness or willingness to forgive is one of the great differences between the Nazi past and the Jewish past and present; between what they, the Nazis, have done to us and would be willing to do again, and how we Jews feel about you.

You must also know that you are not the only one who carries a conscious or unconscious feeling of guilt and shame. I too carry guilt and shame, though not for the same reasons.

We who have survived feel deeply guilty for having survived. Please do not try to find logic in it; the feeling is as irrational as yours. But there it is. We are ashamed to show our wounds to others, especially to you. Why we should feel guilt or shame for having survived, when we have not chosen to be our own executioners, I do not know.

Many books will be written on this subject in years to come. But for the moment I can say that I too share these feelings.

This sense of guilt drives me to seek a purpose for my life that is larger than life itself. Without such a purpose I feel that I would not deserve to live.

So we share guilt for different reasons. You, because of your parents and because you do not know; and I because of your parents and because I am a survivor and I do know. The survivor always feels guilty. The strange thing is that those who really *are* guilty do not seem to feel it at all.

I want to send this letter to you at a stage in my life when I have tried to integrate, absorb and understand the world and the past. I put before you some of my understandings, feelings and thoughts.

I hope you will respond.

Eugene Heimler

8

CHAPTER I

ABOUT MYSELF

I was born four years after the end of World War One. The world, as I perceived it, was safe. Of course I could not have known that it was otherwise. The world is always safe when there are father, mother, family and friends around; familiar faces, familiar surroundings.

Within this safe world the most stable part was my mother. She had an extraordinary gift to stir the depths of my imagination by telling tales and stories during the long evenings of winter and summer. The winters were cozy and warm: inside it was warm, outdoors there was snow which stilled the streets as if people walked on tiptoe everywhere.

In the summer the rooms were darkened so that it was cozy and cool, and mother always had her stories ready. Some of these, I believe, she made up herself. Some were true. Others had been written by her favorite authors. And poems of course, hundreds of them.

In the spring I was allowed to wear ankle socks instead of the kind that came up to my knees. Somewhere around the middle of March – how I longed and looked forward to it! – I could put on my ankle socks. This heralded a new beginning: the arrival of spring.

I was a rather independent child. While I liked to play with others, and did so quite a lot, I liked to be alone too, fancying myself as king or emperor or the general of some huge army. This duality always stayed with me: being with people and being by myself. This aloneness, which is not the same as loneliness, never bothered me; in fact I was looking for it, - always. I suppose it is an essential part of the creative process.

Outside there was a large garden; - perhaps not so large in reality, but to me, as a small child, it seemed so.

We played hide-and-seek in the garden behind the trees and bushes. '*We*', that meant the children from the house and from the neighborhood.

And there was a courtyard, where we played football and ran and rode our little bicycles. I still remember the color of mine: it was red.

Uncles came and aunts came; they stayed for a while, and then they left. As I said, the world was cozy and safe. They brought presents, excitement and stories. I sat on their laps and smelled their tobacco or perfume. The world was safe.

My father would go down to the Continental Coffee-House on the corner and discussed the great issues of the world with his friends. To me all this sounded absolutely marvelous and lovely.

He was a lawyer. In the morning he walked to the courthouse. Then, in the afternoon he came home and worked.

He was a good man, a just and able man, but he was born in a country which did not give him the opportunity to bring his talents to full fruition. I did not as yet understand this.

The world seemed very, very cozy and peaceful.

Our town, Szombathely, was a lovely little place. It was a small town, by any standards, even by Hungarian ones.

It was near the Austrian border. My governess came from Graz or maybe from somewhere in Germany. She taught me a second tongue, which later turned out to be very useful indeed.

There were many things I did not as yet know. The world seemed very lovely and peaceful.

I keep saying these things because I want you to feel the texture of this world of mine in which everything – people, trees, the land itself – exuded an aura of security.

The trees … huge, beautiful chestnut trees. I used to play a lot with those wild chestnuts, making things out of them, polishing them, caressing them. Once I tried to eat them.

"They are very bad for your tummy", Mother said. She seldom stopped me from doing what I wanted.

I had a sister too. She was years older and that means a great deal when a child is small. We had no real contact until I too became an adult.

She was jealous of me for many reasons. And I was jealous of her. She was jealous of me because I was the baby and I was jealous of her because she was the grown-up. As time passed and we both became adults in our own different ways, I began to love her very, very deeply. But at that moment, at the time I am describing, there was a world of distance still between her and me.

There were butterflies in the big park and in the forest beyond the park. The grass, I recall, was tall, almost as tall as I. It was an enchantment to run around there and try to catch a butterfly. I still remember how excited I was. Nowadays I encounter that kind of excitement only in great moments of ecstatic pleasure, in the appreciation of music or art, in an expression on the face of a child or my wife. Oh yes, the world was full of excitement.

As I grew older and went to school I found out that the school my parents sent me to was of a different kind than the one some of the other children attended. They went to Roman Catholic or Protestant or other strangely named schools.

I was sent to what was called the Jewish School. As yet I did not pay too much attention to this. The meaning had not penetrated my mind yet.

Then one day an extraordinary event took place. Wearing longer trousers and a bit taller than before, I was walking to school, when some other boys came by. As I walked past them, wearing my little cap as Jewish boys were supposed to, they pointed toward the Catholic Church with its image of the crucified Jesus and said to me: "Jew boy! You have done it to Him!"

I was deeply shaken and shocked. I looked at the bloodstained man on the cross and asked, "Have I? What have I done?"

11

I went home and asked my mother.

She was rather philosophical about it and tried to play down the whole episode. "Oh, you know, children are stupid. They don't know what they are saying. It's not that important."

Then my father came into the room and joined the conversation. He took it much more seriously. Rarely did such conversations take place between my father and me. Only much, much later, after my mother had died and we were in the middle of World War Two, did we have another such discussion. But on this occasion he turned to me and said: "Jancsi, sit down."

And there I sat and waited. This enormously big man, with blue eyes and light brown hair, stood in front of me like a statue. His face was serious as he asked, "Do you know who Jesus was?"

I said, "No Father, I don't know."

He said, "He was a Jew, like you and I."

I said, "Yes", and waited.

My mother was still in the room. Rather nervously, she said: "Ernest, don't you think he is a little bit young for all this?"

He looked at her with an expression I shall never forget, and said, "No, Maria, for *that* he is not too young. He must know the truth *now* before he learns it from others … the lies, the false accusations."

I felt a thrill. I felt that a drama was enacted right before my eyes; a drama that had its roots somewhere far beyond my understanding.

Beyond my parents somehow there was a dimension still deeper than their own personal thoughts and feelings. Not only was my father speaking to me. It was not only my mother whom I saw reacting to what he said, but something that arose from unfathomed depths and at that time was still nameless. Later I learnt to call it by the name of the '*Unconscious*'. I felt a feeling of unease, anxiety and tension, yet beyond it a sense of beauty too. Fear: yes, that also was a part of it.

My father looked at me, full of love and caring, and said, "Do you know, Jancsi, who you are?"

Now this is a hard question for a six or seven year old boy.

I said, "Yes, Daddy, I know who I am. I am Jancsi."

A little smile, like the sun breaking through the clouds and then withdrawing again, lit up his face as he said, "Yes, Jancsi, you are you. But I have told you that you are also a Jew. We are Jews. Our parents were Jews. Our ancestors were Jews, way back into history. Back, far back into the past."

That feeling of anxiety, tension and fear, and unutterable beauty came again. I knew then that I loved this man even though I often feared him. I loved him deeply.

"What does it mean, Daddy," I asked, "to be a Jew?"

"That you will learn," he said. "For the moment, there is something you must understand. Those bastards told you that *you* killed him. Well, let me tell you something. He was one of our own people. And one day you will understand that *they* killed him.

He was a Jew."

"Yes, Daddy."

"That is all," he said. "You must never allow yourself to believe such lies. Now your mother will tell you more. I must get back to work."

He left me there stunned, astounded, filled with those mixed feelings that come from what I *now* know was the unconscious.

I recall my mother standing there, looking out of the window towards the distant mountains of Koszeg which separated Hungary from Austria. She was a beautiful woman with black hair and black eyes. She turned to me and said, "Of course, as always, your father is right, Jancsi. But there is something he did not tell you. After Jesus was killed, people created a new religion. They called themselves Christians."

"Yes, Mummy?"

"Pali and Gyuszi are Christians. Some of your other friends are Christians. We must not let that stand between them and us. Their parents, grandparents and great-grandparents have lived in this country and in this little town, just as we do. They are no different from us. You can see: they play the same games that you do. They are only different in one sense: that they are Christians. They believe that Jesus was the son of God."

"The son of God?" I asked.

She said, "Yes, they believe that Jesus was the son of God."

"Mummy," I said, "I don't understand what you are talking about."

She smiled again. "Of course not. All I want you to know is that your friends are not like the boys you met in the street. Although they may believe in some other things than you do, basically they are the same as we are. Now go and play."

I think that was the end of it; at least the end of that particular episode which I now recall and which, my young German friend, is perhaps significant for you to know: My first encounter with Christianity started with the cross. A bleeding man on the cross, who was a Jew and, I was told, was the son of God.

As I told you before, I like being alone. During my times of solitude I thought about the man on the cross. I did not like him bleeding there. I did not like it a bit. I would have liked him to stand there on the cross, happy and content and smiling, instead of that terrible expression of agony and torture on his face. And they, those boys, said that I have done that to him. Well, God sees my soul, I did not, and that's all there was to it, and off I went to play football.

That episode was the beginning, not the end, of the story. The world was still safe and peaceful around me. It took a very, very long time before the meaning of it all began to shake my world like an earthquake and before my peace was gone.

My grandmother, whom I loved dearly, had a typical Hungarian peasant accent, and she talked to me a lot about all sorts of things. When I was puzzled or happy or excited I would turn to her because she always answered me frankly. So I spoke to her about Jesus I said, "Grandma, who's this Jesus?"

Her reaction surprised me. Usually she was nice and talkative but now suddenly she became very serious and said: "We do not talk about him."

"Grandma, I *want* to talk about him."

"There are other things to talk about," she said.

I thought this over. Granny was very, very serious. In her rustic Hungarian dialect she was really telling me to shut up and turn the conversation to other topics.

"Our family," I went on, "...Mummy says that we have been living here in Hungary for many generations. Aren't we Hungarians?"

"Yes, we are," she said with pride. "We are Hungarians. So is your father and so was my husband, God bless his soul and memory. And your grandfather and his father, and his father's father ... all the way back through the ages. They were all Hungarians."

"Good," I said, "and before that?"

"Hungarians." she said. "But some time, back somewhere in the centuries, we came from somewhere else."

I hoped that I would not upset my grandmother by asking some questions that she would refuse to answer. So I asked cautiously: "Grandma, where do we come from?"

As she looked at me now, her eyes seemed to mirror a lake or a river and a mountain. She said with great tenderness: "Originally we come from the Land of Israel."

Why tears appeared in her eyes I could not understand.

"The Land of Israel?" I asked.

"Yes."

"A tiny land," she went on, "but it is no more," she added with a sigh. "But if you study your Bible and so you should … have you? Do you?"

"Yes, Grandma, I do." I did not tell her that I failed to understand the Hebrew words. I could translate them, but not relate them to what Granny was talking about. Not yet anyway: I did not understand anything about the Land of Israel, even though the Bible indeed referred to it.

"The Land of Israel …," she said with tears in her eyes, "God promised that one day we shall go back there."

"Why?" I said. "We are Hungarians."

"Yes, we are Hungarians. But when the hour comes, and the Messiah comes, we shall all go back to where we originally came from; - to the Land of Israel."

Now I saw the tears trickling down her cheeks. I had touched upon something deep within her.

She said: "You know that I am the descendant of a prince?"

I became very excited. "Granny, Granny, a prince?"

"Yes," she said, "I have royal blood in my veins, at least, the blood of princes."

I looked at her and could easily envisage her with a crown on her head.

"Yes, Grandma." With her thick Hungarian peasant accent and dialect she might really be a queen or a princess. Indeed she might.

"Granny, tell me about it!"

"We, when we" –remember, my German friend, she said 'we'! – "left the Land of Israel thousands of years ago, one of your ancestors, a man called Abarbanel, was a doctor, and he became physician to one of the kings of Spain. And the king trusted this ancestor of yours so much that he made him a prince; a duke, I believe. And I am a direct descendant of this man. And you have that princely blood within you too."

'This I've got to tell Pali and Gyuszi and the rest! I've got to tell all my friends!'

16

"Then I'm a prince too, aren't I?"

Granny smiled. "No, not quite; a prince you are not. But you are a member of a priestly people."

"Priestly?"

"Yes, a people of priests. We Jews are a priestly people."

My confusion grew apace. The hooligans told me that I have killed Jesus. My father tells me something about who I am and that I must not believe their charge. (I didn't anyway, yet part of me was disturbed: the man was bleeding, and I don't like men associated with blood and pain.) My mother says this and that. My Grandma doesn't want to talk about Jesus. I come from a princely family. And now, *now* I learn that I belong to a people of priests. I did not even quite know what priests were.

So I simply left it at that, as children usually do when they get tired. The shadows began to grow long outside and it seemed as though the trees were saying: "Jancsi, go and have a little nap." And there, by the side of my snoring grandmother, I fell asleep. And that was that.

As I was growing into adolescence and adulthood, I did all the things that most of the others did too. I was told that I had been an extremely naughty child. In fact, I was so naughty that I became famous for it. In later years I met people who, on hearing my name, exclaimed, "Ah, so you were the naughty Jancsi who did this, that or the other!"

Yes, I was a very naughty child. Not malicious but full of mischief. Yet my mother's control over me was never very strict.

Once I had a fight in the garden; I cannot recall whether we were fighting for fun or in earnest, but it was a fight all right. I was still pretty small then. A child hit me in the eye, maybe with a stick or some leaves, I no longer remember; but for a moment or two I could not see. I was terribly frightened and ran upstairs crying. Mother listened carefully. Her solution to the problem was not 'why?' or 'what?' or 'how?', but saying, "Go to the toilet and take a pee!" And off I went

17

obediently to the toilet and peed. And that was the end of it. She didn't tell me "You are a naughty boy. You shouldn't fight. What have you been fighting about?" She just said: "Go and take a pee!"

So the solution to great problems was some kind of activity, and peeing was a pretty basic one. Well, thus I learnt questions must lead to action.

I was quite good at school. But some of my teachers found it odd when I asked questions like "Is there life on other planets? And if there is, how do we know that there is, and if there isn't, how do we know that there isn't?" Such questions made my teachers nervous. "There isn't," they would say. And I said: "Well, how do you know that there isn't?" "Jancsi shut your mouth!"

Instead of keeping quiet, such answers made me excited and keen to know more. And I went to books, to read, to find out. Not just about the world beyond our world; not only about the moon and the stars and God and Israel, but everything I could lay my hands on. Hungarian history was one of these subjects. Whatever I could read, I read, voraciously. As yet I did not know what to do with what I had read. There were mysteries in this world. Cracks appeared in my peace. There were Jews and there were Christians. There was a word called 'anti-Semitism' which I could not quite figure out.

The arrival of sexuality added to all the mysteries that were beginning to shake up my world.

While I was growing up, these two mysteries, - being a Jew and sexuality - coming from the deepest core of my being, affected me, challenged and assailed me. As the years went on I tried to solve these problems, yet neither reading nor thinking led me to understanding or solutions.

I must confess that my teachers who tried to instill Judaism in me did not make a very good job of it. They spoke of and interpreted Judaism in purely ritual terms. They taught us what you may or may not eat; what you could or could not do on the Sabbath, the day of rest; how you must pray and things like that.

Such doctrines did not touch that essential beauty which arose from the depth of my being – along with fear and tension – when my father spoke to me on that memorable occasion about being a Jew.

The meaning of Judaism came to me more from experience than from instruction. It was an ancient custom and law that on Yom Kippur, the Day of Atonement, you forgave the wrongs others had done to you and asked for forgiveness for the wrongs you had done to them. And you had to forgive yourself too, because there could be no forgiveness without facing yourself first.

When I saw adults with tears in their eyes, begging forgiveness from one another, *that*, yes *that* impressed me profoundly. The atmosphere at the service on Yom Kippur, as I stood before the Almighty God of Israel, asking Him for forgiveness and feeling in my heart that if I truly meant what I prayed for I should indeed be forgiven; - yes, that too meant a great deal to me.

What I could never understand, however, and for that question there was no clear answer anywhere, was this: Why have we been persecuted down the centuries? Why the blood libels, the torture, the inquisitions, the pogroms, the incessant pain? Why?

It took me many, many years and many, many struggles to even begin to find answers to these questions. And whatever answers I found, they were never complete.

I want you to know that I could easily have become my own persecutor. In 1492 the *Holy Inquisition* in Spain culminated in the expulsion of the Jews from that land. They began their journey northward, away from the Mediterranean Sea, which was their only connecting link with their ancient land. They moved up across France into the Netherlands, where some of them settled and established flourishing, peaceful communities. The Dutch welcomed them, gave them safety and protection. Some moved on into Germany.

Documentary evidence shows that my ancestors settled near Augsburg where they became farmers working on the land. It is not quite clear at what point, but one part of the family accepted the Christian faith, converting to Roman Catholicism. The other part, - it is also uncertain just when, - moved on towards Hungary. The descendants of the German branch still reside there, still in the same area. Some of them were Nazis and Nazi sympathizers. Their offspring still lives there today. Had I been born into the German branch, I would be writing a different story today. I might have become my own persecutor. I could have become my own executioner.

I say all this to you, my young German friend, so that you know that I do not see things in black and white. I cannot point an accusing finger at anyone. I truly do not know what I would have done if I had been born and raised in your country, as it so easily might have been the case. But as it happened, I was born in Hungary, a Jew. That is where my branch of the family settled, near the Austrian border. They too became farmers, an unusual kind of occupation for Jews. I have in my possession documents that show a family tree which reaches back into the seventeen hundreds. This journey to Hungary must have taken place some time in the sixteen hundreds.

I do not point a finger of accusation at anyone, in any direction, except in the direction of human experience.

I want to show you what it means to be a Jew, because most Christians, including Germans, never understood this since they were exposed only to the Nazi propaganda machine and before that to the anti-Semitic teachings of the Church.

Let me now return to my personal story and tell you that despite the internal struggles and bafflements I managed to grow into a man by the time the Second World War broke out.

The internal and external events of those years, and particularly the year which I spent in Auschwitz and Buchenwald and some other concentration camps, I described in my book *Night of the Mist*. Of the subsequent events of my life following the war, I wrote in my book titled *A Link in the Chain*. I do not want to repeat here what I have already dealt with. But I must make some reference to the essentials of what happened after 1939. I do so because I want to introduce myself to you completely.

After the Nazi occupation of Austria on March 11, 1938, the mood in Hungary changed. The Hungarian Nazis were encouraged to crawl out of the woodwork. So were the Nationalists, the chauvinists, the fascists too. Practically overnight, we became an open target to anyone who wanted to attack.

My father's generation regarded this as the most natural thing in the world. For us, young men and women, such things seemed far from natural. We rebelled because part of growing up is rebellion. But how could our rebellion express itself?

We aligned ourselves with leftist ideals or with ideals that came from Palestine where a great struggle was taking place in order to establish a Jewish national home. The holy books, - the Bible, the Talmud, our prayers - , constantly refer to Eretz Yisrael, the Land of Israel, to which we shall one day return. In the midst of persecution, suspicion and hatred we faced east, towards Jerusalem, and identified ourselves with what was promised to be ours.

Some of us were on the left of the Zionist movement, some at the centre, some on the right, and some on the extreme right. This was the only way in which our rebellion could find expression.

Hungary was a strange country. It permitted all this. Some sort of Parliament was still functioning. Parties still had some freedom. There was still some freedom of the press. There was still some freedom of assembly. Zionism was certainly not discouraged.

It was here, within the Jewish community, that my first attempts at writing poetry found an audience. They acknowledged me as a poet. My poems were published in the local paper as well and then, just about at the time of the outbreak of World War Two, my first book was published. My books sold well; some of the poems became quite popular.

By now I was thirsting for the ideas of Judaism, without belonging to any extreme. Having come to understand the *message* that Judaism has given to us as well as to the world, I was determined not to give in, not to give up, but to fight on; and one day, if I survived, to hand on this *message*.

The Nazis accused us of poisoning society with our ideas which were totally alien to Aryan thinking and race. And so they were and so they are indeed.

Three thousand years ago we had a Supreme Court sitting in Jerusalem, concerning itself with the dignity of human life, creating legal processes unprecedented at that time anywhere in the world. Remember that at that time in England, in Germany, in the rest of the world, people were still practically cannibals.

The Sanhedrin, the Supreme Court, was also a kind of Parliament with seventy members who decided on law, trials and such matters. They were concerned with the dignity of life, never about the purity of race. Many people of foreign background were allowed to blend into the Jewish people and faith, and were accepted as equals.

They spoke of the value of life, of tolerance, not only in speech but in action. Thousands of years ago, as you will see later, they established the first welfare state in Judea and Israel. Part of the harvest of a landlord belonged to the poor and the needy, to the orphan and the widow and the stranger.

Physically handicapped or mentally ill people were kept in what nowadays we would call hostels or hospitals. The Romans, when they entered Jerusalem, described with scorn

22

the way the Jews cherished cripples instead of killing them. Indeed we were poison when viewed from a purely Aryan perspective.

Our prophets dreamed of a world in which all people were united. No supremacy of one nation over others, but rather the unity of all nations in one truth.

The Nazis proclaimed the supremacy of the Aryan race, with all others viewed as inferior. They accused us of greed, of using Christians and Christian money to build our own fortunes.

Read history, my young friend, and you will find that at times the kings and princes of Christian Europe forced Jews into these unpopular roles of money lenders and tax collectors. True enough, when the chips were down, money represented the only safety for some of my ancestors. With some justification they felt that with money they could ransom their lives. But in Hungary, where my people had been living for centuries, this was a very strange and alien notion. I, for one, have never been exposed to it. Neither, as far as I know, were my friends.

In the Nazi eyes we were poison, a poison that had to be eliminated from the structure of society. That way society might survive.

If you go to the books of history you will find that our only sin consisted in introducing humanitarian and ethical ideals into the world which the world finds difficult even today to accept.

As a group of people, we are no different from any other when it comes to selfishness or self-sacrifice. That goes without saying. As a nation, Israel is no better and no worse than any other nation. Yet, in one sense, we were and are different. We have something deeply in common. The experience of persecution has pushed us together as a huddle of frightened people, determined people, faithful people.

A Jew does not speak a great deal about God. In fact, it is forbidden even to mention His name. He is invisible, unthinkable and unimaginable. But He is. He is there in the trees, in the world, in every single creature that has been created. He is behind every thought and every action, beyond desire, beyond the relationship of men and women.

We were accused of plotting against the Christian world, either as Communists or as Capitalists. What nonsense! The Jewish Communist and the Jewish Capitalist had the same gap between them as any other Communist and Capitalist anywhere in the world. There could never be any organized plot because it was simply impossible. Jews were not a nation of plotters; they were a nation of dreamers.

On March 19th, 1944, the armies of the Third Reich invaded Hungary from Austria and occupied the country. There was no resistance. The nation was unprepared. Then the usual sequence of persecution started: yellow stars, ghettoes, and eventually the crematoria.

I spent one year facing the enemy and experiencing the ultimate degradation a human being can endure. Yet I survived. I emerged from the camps injured, bearing both physical and mental wounds. But I survived, and as time passed I have learnt to put some of those injuries to useful purpose.

I also brought memories with me from the camps. Memories of horrors, of unbelievable cruelty, perpetrated not only by the Nazis and by the Gestapo against us, but also by prisoners against one another. Yet I brought also memories of shining human courage, compassion and love. I brought with me an awareness of the myth of race and nationality, and the knowledge that as mankind we are one. Buchenwald for example was a grand Internationale of most European nations. We all suffered the same blows and dreamed the same dreams.

Broken, but alive I returned to Hungary to start a new life, to make a new beginning. I was married before. My young wife was killed, consumed in the ovens of Auschwitz. I married again. I pulled up my roots and put them down again, this time in England. I have lived there since 1947. It is from there that I travel abroad in order to learn and teach.

But for the moment let me just say this: once the ultimate price had been paid, life is a gift. And it seems that I have paid the ultimate price. My family of birth has been wiped out, as well as most of my friends. But I created a new family and made new friends. And with these memories, experiences and agonies I began to shape a philosophy of life which is very real to me indeed.

I can sum it up very briefly:

"There is no defeat. And if you do feel defeat, it can be turned into victory."

This is what my life is all about. And this is what I would like to share with you.

CHAPTER II

AN EXPERIENCE OF JUDAISM

In the Judean desert, surrounded by hills, an old woman wept with longing for a child. Her childbearing days were well over, and her husband was very, very old indeed. Then one day a miracle happened to the woman and her husband: Despite her age, she conceived a child. And that child became the first Jew ever born. The father's name was Abraham, the mother's name was Sarah, and the child's name was Isaac.

Then, having gone through the agonies and hopelessness of being without issue and the subsequent miracle and joy of parenthood, Abraham is commanded by God to give up his only son as a sacrifice, the son, born through a miracle.

Abraham took the boy to Mount Moriah and was about to sacrifice him in accordance with the word of the Lord. But at the last moment God and His angels stopped him. He was promised that the child would be the forefather, the beginning of a great nation.

As a child I was deeply affected by this story, for many reasons.

First, there is the element of miracle. Yes, that had an extraordinary impact on my mind. Here were a woman of ninety and a man of ninety-nine. How could they even dare to think of having a child? Yet, it did happen. That aspect of the story always filled me with joy and a sense of mystery. But after all that, how can God ask for the ultimate sacrifice of these people who, at an advanced stage of their lives, managed to bring forth the child they had always longed for? How could He ask them to give up this child? And yet, that precisely was demanded.

This request gave me a fear and an anxiety, an uncertainty about the intentions of God.

Then the father took his trusting young son up the mountain, and the child asked: "Where is the victim for the sacrifice?" And the father said: "God will provide it in good time." And then the boy found out that he himself was to be the sacrifice.

I was terrified.

And then, at the very last moment, just as the knife rose high to execute the outrageously cruel command, it was stopped, and a covenant was made to bind all as yet unborn generations.

To put it in a nutshell: herein lies the history and destiny of my people. But beyond the history and destiny of a nation, there lies that other part, which concerns God Himself and man himself.

Man must have a dream, however impossible. He must ask for the fulfillment of the dream, and then it is granted. And when it is granted, a *test* comes; a period of testing, to see whether he can measure up to the dream. The test can be exceedingly severe, almost harsh enough to destroy the dream itself. Yet, when you come to the very limit of your desperation, at that very instant, not only is the dream ultimately fulfilled, but a treasured covenant is established, which makes the dream permanent.

Within this dream, fulfillment, test and eternal contract lies Jewish destiny and my peoples' philosophy, and my own personal philosophy too.

This I know: without the dream there cannot ever be reality. The dream comes first. But I am ready and prepared. I am almost all the time waiting for the test to come, for the time when the sheep are separated from the goats. The time when we can show what kind of stuff we are made of.

Oh, anyone can dream. That is easy. Even the miracle is not all that impossible. But it is the testing that most people fail.

27

And I say to you: Jewish destiny lies in the testing; because after the testing comes the Covenant, the eternal contract between Israel and God.

Most peoples have failed the test. Nations once great, that subjugated us, are not even on the map any more. Babylon, the greatest power on earth at one time, is nowhere. Rome, the mighty empire, that ruled practically the whole known world, - nowhere. The Third Reich, whose professed ambition was to last a thousand years, - nowhere.

And we, God's people, still exist, although our ranks have been reduced by persecution, inquisitions and the Holocaust. We are still around. We shall be around until the end of days.

He said: "I make a covenant with you and with your seed, and with your children's until the end of time."

He said: "I give you this land, the Land of Israel" ... again and again and again.

But first, individually and collectively, we must pass the test, endure the ordeal.

What frightened me was the test. How easily the knife could have plunged into my heart, as it in fact did to millions. Six million died in our own time and age. Only a few, I among them, survived;

Yet, in my own generation I saw the rebirth of the State of Israel.

Again, after the ultimate testing, the triumph of the dream.

Judaism has a collective as well as an individual dimension of survival. Individuals come and go, live and die, but Israel endures. It endures despite the designs of its persecutors.

Individuals -six million of them- paid the ultimate sacrifice in order to awaken the world's conscience and thus enable the impossible, the unparalleled to happen in history.

A modern miracle is being enacted in front of our own eyes A scattered people returning from all over the globe and out of the dust and destruction recreating their country. Israel interweaves religion with peoplehood and nationhood.

28

If you asked me: "Where do you belong?" Fifty years ago I would have answered: "I belong to Hungary."

If you asked me the question while I was in the concentration camp, I would have replied: "I belong to a persecuted people".

If you ask me now, I say: "I am a British Citizen." I love this country, Great Britain, its history, Parliament, democracy. And I would really make the ultimate sacrifice for her. I swore allegiance to the Crown. I am a British citizen. I have a British passport.

You might ask again: "Doesn't this conflict with the 'we' you kept talking about, with your belonging to a nation that is Israel?"

My answer is: "Now just wait a moment! I belong to Judaism and to the Jewish people. I am not an Israeli citizen."

And yet, at the moment I say this, there is a rift in my heart. Though I am not a citizen of Israel, what happens there day by day, week by week, affects me more deeply than anything else I can think of.

What am I then? Am I a split person with several loyalties? No. I do not have several loyalties.

If Britain asked me to fight for her, I would do so, because I believe in the ideal she represents, especially in this age of dictatorships rampant throughout the world.

If you asked: "Would you also fight for Israel?" I would answer: "Yes." And yet, I am not a citizen of Israel; I am a Jew.

I am searching within my heart for an answer to this dilemma. Yet, it is not really a dilemma at all. You see, my allegiance is not just to Israel, a political state recreated in the twentieth century, reborn out of a persistent belief sustained over millennia. No, my allegiance is not to a political state, but to the words of the Bible, of God, Who promised this land to my ancestors thousands of years ago, and the promise was for all generations to come.

Listen to me, my friend! It is not this land, not even the fields, not even the dazzling transformation of the desert into

29

a garden. It is not the Judean hills, or the wilderness, or the cities.

It is Jerusalem. Jerusalem, the Golden. Jerusalem, the Holy.

And even that, not as a miracle of architecture, unique in time and in eternity. Jerusalem embodies an idea that was born there, invisible, yet pervading the world to its foundations. So deep is it that there is practically no nation, no people unaffected by it, by its Law, order, justice, and humanity.

You say, all this sounds too idealistic, that it cannot possibly be true. Surely, there must be some negative side to the story, an obverse side to the coin? Indeed there is.

You see, I am a Jew, whether I like it or not. Yet I do not obey all the 613 commandments that I am supposed to fulfill each day. These commandments are seen as utterly binding by the very pious, who regard them as the revealed word of God.

I myself heed the spirit beyond the letter of the Law. Yet despite my failure to carry out all the commandments, I am a Jew. I am a Jew because my mother was a Jew. I am a Jew because I belong to the Jewish People through the long chain of historic experience. I am a Jew because as a Jew I believe in God. I am a Jew because I am circumcised.

Circumcised? What does that have to do with it?

What does my penis have to do with my being a Jew and with God?

To Gentile ears it may sound like sacrilege to say that my penis reminds me of my contract with God. What I do with my penis also reminds me of my Covenant with the God of Israel and of the Universe.

Please understand this! It is very significant. It explains a great deal about freedom on the one hand and about fear on the other.

Imagine, if you will, a Bedouin tent in the desert. Oh, those black tents are still around, in the Negev and elsewhere in Israel and outside Israel. Wandering tribes put up their tents here and there, and then move on.

One day, one hour, one moment, almost four thousand years ago, something extraordinary happened to some nomads in the wilderness. A vision came to an old man..

God appeared to Abraham and said to him:

"I am God Almighty. Walk before me and be whole hearted. And I will make a covenant between Me and you and I will increase you greatly."

Do I really believe all this, near the end of the twentieth century? In an age when man can go into space? When man has already stepped onto the moon and is about to visit distant stars. And has the hydrogen bomb, and fast air travel and central heating, and an oil crisis?

Do I, Eugene Heimler, really believe this? That thousands of years ago, God appeared to an old man named Abram - his name was not as yet Abraham -? Do I believe that?

Yes, I do. And if you will go on reading my story, then, I hope, you too will believe it, for one simple reason: Because in certain more modern forms these very apparitions, these same communications can happen to you too, if only you can open the door of your soul and if only you keep an open mind.

You might ask: "Do I have to be a Jew for such communications to take place?"

"No, you do not have to be a Jew for that. But it so happens that this occurred to a man who became the first Jew and whose son was the first born Jew.

"You will be my people", He said.

You might ask, "What is the other side, the negative side, of all this? You speak of ethics, of values, of awe and beauty. You talk as though there was nothing wrong."

My answer, my young German friend, is this:

"You know pretty well what was wrong. It was that we died like flies throughout the centuries;. That our lives and deaths were at the mercy of others until quite recently when we resurrected and recreated our own State."

31

You might ask: "As a Gentile, a Christian, am I better or worse than you, because God appeared to your ancestor, Abraham, and made a covenant with him?"

I say to you: "You are no better and no worse than I am, as a person. But I cannot help the fact that the Covenant was made with Abraham and Isaac and Jacob and since I am their seed, with me too."

Let me go back to circumcision and its relationship with God. This is a topic you are unlikely to have considered before. You may even have been brought up to see some contradiction in this matter.

"You shall be circumcised in the flesh of your foreskin, and it shall be a symbol of the Covenant between Me and you." (Genesis 17, 11)

Here it is. The instruction is — and please note the present tense 'is' – binding, and it implies that circumcision, the removal of the foreskin of the male penis, is the sign of the Covenant between God and me. This fills me with extraordinary feelings of fear, joy, and importance. I shall tell you why.

The penis is the source of life. It carries the seed. At moments of desire and climax it serves as a conscious as well as an unconscious reminder that there is an agreement between Him and me, and that I must remain true to certain values even within the very relationship with the woman with whom I am 'making love'; that I have a responsibility. I cannot help it; it is there. But beyond the responsibility there is something else.

Consciously or unconsciously, every time I relive the fear I have experienced at my circumcision on the eighth day of my life, when that event could have been the end of me.

The Covenant of circumcision is a very dangerous thing. God chose well, in designating this as the ultimate symbol of the bond between God and Israel, because this is the male's most vulnerable part. The moment of love and sexuality is also a moment that can end our life at any instant at His will.

Now I believe that God chose this sign of the Covenant because He knew, that in the relationship of man and woman, which produces life, deep feelings, poetry (some of our Jewish kings and psalmists have sung of it since the dawn of history), unutterable beauty and pleasure, there is also an act of union with Him involved. I say "Him", because the masculine gender is used to describe God. Yet He also refers to Himself as *"I Am That Which I Am"* ... and then all is mystery, ineffable and transcendent. So even "Him" is not adequate.

I do not believe that God is either male or female.

God is. *"I am that which I am".*

My sexual organ is the symbol of my ongoing relationship with God. It is therefore perhaps the most important and powerful driving force in human life.

"Your seed". He continually talks about the future. And He continues to talk about the importance of the seed. And the penis is its vehicle.

Many other explanations have been given to the act of circumcision, but let me simply say that whether a Jew is extremely religious or wholly irreligious, this ritual he will want to perform upon his male children on the eighth day of their life, unless the baby is ill, in which case it is postponed. The Hebrew term for the covenant of circumcision is *"Brit Milah"*. Sometimes it is referred to as *"Brit Avraham"*, which means "the Covenant of Abraham".

Originally, when tribal customs still prevailed, the father, as head of the clan, performed the circumcision of the infant himself. Later on this function was transferred to the so-called *"mohel"*, whose special skills enabled him to perform the act with perfect precision, which even Gentile physicians have generally admired.

At this point, as a culmination of this extraordinary ceremony, the child receives his Hebrew name.

Then the father chants the prayer: "As he has entered the Covenant so may he be privileged to enter upon the study of the Torah, and under the marriage canopy of 'chuppa', and the performance of good deeds."

I was given the name of Mordecai, and because my father's name was Aharon, I am Mordecai ben Aharon, Mordecai, the son of Aaron. And so my son was given a name which includes my own name. And right across the generations, from the patriarch Abraham to this moment, father and son are always linked together.

Throughout history the different nations, some of which, as I told you, are extinct by now, recognized that in reality circumcision has been the one main cause that kept Jewish identity alive. That is why kings and emperors forbade Jews to circumcise their children. And such laws and decrees have been widely and persistently defied by Jews.

In a major work on the Jewish religion, *Judah Halevi*, the poet-philosopher of twelfth century Spain, writes:

"Circumcision has nothing to do with the constitution of social life. Yet Abraham, although this commandment seems to go against nature, and although he was a hundred years old, subjected his own person as well as his son to it. Thus it became the symbol of the covenant, by which the Divine Power is linked with him and his descendants."

CHAPTER III

THE TRIAL (1958)
(An inquisition in modern times)

I want you to feel, my young friend, something about the inner world. Not just the past. Not just the past of a child, who grew up with certain values, ideas and ethics. Not just what grandmother said and father said and mother said and did, or what the child read and how it affected him.

This time I want to come very near to you, body and soul. This book cannot be, must not be, merely a form of instruction for Gentiles, for Christians, for young Germans, even for you, my friend. That surely is not my aim.

The story which follows was told to me by a friend, who was also a survivor of the holocaust; I wrote it down thirty-three years ago. It is entitled "The Trial". The trial of a middle-aged Jew, who falls in love with …

Just read the story.

The place was shrouded in darkness; only the candles flickered on the platform above. There were three candles. Sometimes the wind blew from somewhere, the lights trembled, and the three shadows also trembled on the wall.

Jonathan looked at the judges and thought, "I know this place. I have been here before." But however hard he tried, he just could not work out where and when he had witnessed this ghastly scene, and seen the three judges high above him. He was tired of kneeling, and he knew that he had to kneel because that was the law of the place. Again he questioned how he knew. He knew. That was all.

The judge was an old man. Jonathan felt he was too old, perhaps eighty or ninety- old, anyway. He wore a funny wig, the kind judges do in court, and Jonathan was a little annoyed about all this formality. Yes, everything was too theatrical.

The Attorney sat on the left; he had a strange, womanish face. For a while he thought the Attorney was a woman, but when he spoke, it was a man's voice, a hard voice; it sounded rather unpleasant. On the right hand side sat the Defender. He was a much younger man with a smile on his face, and Jonathan wished to God he did not smile all the time. But he did.

"It is our custom to complete our cases before the candles burn out", the Judge now addressed Jonathan and added: "Do you understand?"

By now he was slightly annoyed. The old man must take him for an idiot: what was there so hard to understand? He said:

"Yes, my Lord, I understand."

"Good", said the Judge, "we must make our rules clear, mustn't we?"

He looked at the candles. The middle one, placed in front of the Judge, had burnt down further than the other two. 'How long does it take for candles to burn?' he mused. 'I suppose it depends on thickness and length. How long did those candles take to burn out at home in Prague, those candles, lights of a bygone age, bygone Sabbath nights? How beautiful mother's face was by the light of those candles! Where is mother now?"

"Is your name Jonathan Rulph?"

"Yes, my Lord, it is."

"Isn't it a rather unusual name for a foreigner?"

"I am sorry, my Lord, that is my name."

"Were you born in Prague in 1920?"

"Yes, my Lord, I was."

The judge was thinking. He turned to the Attorney and said:

"Strangely enough, I can remember that night, the 12th of March 1920. It was snowing; the wind kept blowing bits of paper against the window. A cold year, a very long winter, a very chilly spring!" The Attorney answered: "Yes, your Lordship."

"Jonathan Rulph, you were born on a cold night. Did you know?"

"My mother told me exactly the same, my Lord."

"You were a second child, weren't you? The first one was also a son. He was a few years older."

"That is correct, my Lord, three years older."

The judge said: "You may stand now." Jonathan stood up and faced his judges. The old man looked at the papers before him. He seemed to be searching for something. When he found what he was looking for, he looked at the accused again.

"You father, wasn't he called Roth? Cyril Roth?"

"No, your Lordship, that was my grandfather. My father was called Anthony Rulph."

"Oh yes, of course, of course. These candles, they don't give much light, do they?"

The old judge indeed knew the routine, and had his case well prepared. That's right: Jonathan's father was a vet, a quite unusual profession for a Jew. He was also a godly man. He went to synagogue every Saturday morning, afternoon and evening. The rest of the time he attended to sick animals. On Friday nights the candles were lit, and Mr. Rulph senior would sit in his study and read the Bible. He would fall asleep, then wake up, and pretend that he had been awake all the time. The judge went on: "You grew up as a Jew; am I right?"

"Quite right, your Lordship."

"Will you now swear on the Old Testament that the evidence you will give is the truth, the whole truth, and nothing but the truth?"

"So help me God!"

"Good", said the judge, "good".

With shaking fingers the old Judge lifted a cross and looked at it for some time. He raised the cross; its shadow kept growing ever longer against the wall. In the silence Jonathan could hear his own heart beating.

37

"You see this?" The cross was by now huge upon the wall.

"Yes, my Lord, I see it."

"What is it? Name it!"

"It's a cross, my Lord."

"It is a cross," said the judge quietly, "it is a cross."

Jonathan did not understand. Why does the old man hold the cross for such an infinite length of time while the candles are relentlessly burning down? Every moment is precious, and the trial has hardly begun.

"We must keep in mind now," the Judge went on, still holding the cross, "that Man suffered death upon this cross, and gained new life upon this cross. It may seem irrelevant to you, Jonathan Rulph, but it is relevant to the case. Do you understand?"

Now he really felt like an imbecile. He did not understand.

"I am a Jew, my Lord," and added, "as you know."

"Oh yes," said the Judge, "I know it all right."

Jonathan became aware of an ever increasing uneasiness in his heart. At first it was just a slight trembling, but it grew apace like a sudden storm. Like the shadow of the cross upon the wall. He was relieved to see the judge put the cross down, yet the uneasiness remained. He now felt that the trial would not be as easy as he had hoped.

"In an ordinary case," said the Judge, still looking at the cross before him," I would read the charge to you. But you know the charge. In an ordinary case, the Accuser would accuse and the Defender defend, but you are your own accuser and your own defender. These gentlemen are only here in order to *witness* your case. They will not interfere at any point during this case, only at the very end. Then they will speak; but not before."

Darkness descended on the hall with doubled heaviness, and with it came wind and cold and night. Fog too was seeping in. Through the haze he heard the voice:

"The first candle is your defense. When it burns out I shall tell you to stop. The second candle is your accusation. And the third ... we shall see. Now, Jonathan Rulph, proceed with your defense!"

"I am grateful to you, my Lord, for allowing me to start with my defense. It is so much easier to start with love, with desire, with happiness. I met Elizabeth eight months ago. I met her at Earl's Court Station, to be exact. There was a big crowd; it was the rush hour. The crush forced us to stand face to face in the train, yet our eyes did not meet as yet. My Lord, the train roared on and I felt drawn to her like a nail to a vast magnet. I could not but feel a new sun rising inside me. I said to myself I was mad. In recent years I have often thought, my Lord, that love has evaded me, just as the rain had evaded the fields that summer. Often, during my lonely hours I was wondering if indeed there was such a miracle as true love on this earth. And I realize that it sounds worse than strange, yet I say: for the first time since I stepped ashore on this green island, there was love in that fast moving train of the Circle Line. I also knew that she shared this love with me. I sensed that this meeting of ours had naturalness and inevitability. I reached for her hand and, despite the tight pressure of the throng around us, managed to lift it to my lips and kiss it with a tenderness befitting not a mere hand but some holy book given by God to the world to cherish. And it was only then that I looked into her eyes and saw the blueness of the sea and beyond it the strange life of the abyss. She wept, my Lord, She wept. So help me God.

How can I describe her to you? Is she beautiful? No, she is not, yet to me she is. Her hair fell over her eyes. In the draught of the racing train her blondness moved as the trees move in a storm; she had a little red pimple on the tip of her nose. Right there, amazing! She was almost as tall as I, at least five foot seven. Her eyebrows met in the middle although she no doubt made attempts to shave a gap between them. I told you that she is beautiful. She held my hand, and it was altogether sad and beautiful and stupid and real. We rode round and round the Inner Circle while people were pushing forward to alight and others entered. Suddenly it was quiet. I said, "You can't be more than twenty-four." She smiled through her silly tears and in an accent I could not immediately place she said, "You are quite right. Does it matter?"

At last we got off the train; I don't know how and why, but we did. We walked in Hyde Park until the sun died in the sky and the moon came to play hide-and-seek behind the clouds. We said little and left much unsaid. Then slowly rain came, and slowly we moved towards the lights of the West End.

Neither on that night, my Lord, nor on any subsequent night, did I know her as a man knows a woman. Time has to be ripe, the stars have to be in a certain constellation in the sky; fate has to have the final word.

When morning came I looked out through my window in Highgate. There was no sun, only clouds. Then the postman came with a registered letter.

Only then, my Lord, did I want to know more about her, her habits, her past. How stupid of us to want to know, as if the knowledge of daylight could ever match the knowledge of the night! It was a Saturday morning – I shall never forget -, and as I was reading the letter, I asked her, "Where do you come from?" She could not hear me, so I kissed her eyes and said playfully: "Blue Sea, tell me the secret of your home."

Then, my Lords, she spoke. She only said one word, but that word shattered my peace. That single word, she whispered into my ear, brought forth storms of hitherto unknown ferocity, sleepless nights, visions and nightmares".

Jonathan now looked at the candle that was guttering towards extinction. He looked terrified, for his defense was at an end. And the Judge spoke: "No more, my son. The light is out."

40

With trembling hands the old man lit another candle and said with great sadness: "Jonathan Rulph, now present the charge against you."

When I heard that word, I covered my ears. I wanted to hear no more. But the word, like some snake, burrowed deeper and deeper with its ugly head, and there was no escape. The word she whispered with the honey of love on her lips.

When I heard that word, thunder and lightening flashed across my sky. My love was dead. Hate, huge as a mountain, now weighed on my heart. My lips no longer wanted to kiss her but to tear her apart. My hands now yearned to uproot and to destroy. My eyes that had beheld the submerged miracles of the sea now saw only the fires of hell. I cried. Like a child lost on a cold night, I wept, as I had often wept in my mother's soft, sheltering arms, and I howled at her: "Out! Out, you bitch, you murderer!"

And the word she had whispered to me, my Lords, the word that started all this conflagration, was *Düsseldorf*. "*Düsseldorf*", she had whispered with her ugly bloodstained lips, "*Düsseldorf*", she whined into my ears with a hiss like that of the snake in the Garden of Eden. And then, my Lords, I saw the sharp edge of a knife and I saw her wallowing in her Aryan blood, dead on my spotless bed. And when she saw the knife raised high in my hand, she screamed: "Why? Why, my love?" She did not scream: "No, no!" or "Help!" What she screamed was: "Why?"

I said to her:

"Once I had a mother, whose arms were soft and who held me on cold nights when fears lurked in dark corners. On the 3rd of June, 1943, she was dragged from her home and killed by gas in a place called Auschwitz. You have killed her. You have! I had a father, a quiet man, who lived only for animals and for God. True, he was too busy to set an example of manhood to me. True, too, that he raised his hands to me

41

often during my turbulent years. Yet he was a man of peace, who one morning stood on a mountain-top beside me and said: 'Never forget how good it is for a man to speak up!' This man, who taught me to speak the truth on that mountain-top, you kicked him down the stairs, and as he lay there helpless, writhing in agony, you came and kicked him to death.

"I had a wife, whose love was like the spring; not yet ripe, but full of warm promise. We married young, not knowing what marriage was all about, and we made love as if it were a game. She carried a child in her body, a child whose heart beat in the night, who moved and hoped to see the light of day, - but you made her work in a factory until the day her unborn child could be seen through the torn rags and then you injected her with air ... I had my people, six million of them, and you killed them all."

Then, my Lord, she knelt before me, and pointing towards her golden cross she cried: "Don't, don't go on, Jonathan, my love; I too am crucified." Then, my Lords, she told me a tale, the true tale of her life. She was born on a farm. Her father left her behind as he went off to kill Jews. Yes, my Lords, she did not hide the truth from me, she screamed it aloud: 'He was a brute towards you, Jonathan, and he was a brute towards me too.' She grew up and searched for love, for the love that was denied her. 'My mother', she cried, 'left me on the farm, and when I was twelve the farmer took me and made a woman out of me, amidst pain and wounds. When my mother came home and asked me why I was trembling in the man's presence, I lied. I knew she would not care.'"

She held up the cross in front of her just as you did, my Lord, against the yellow candle lights. And then, my Lord, I fell onto the ground and cursed the moment when I was born. I wept, my Lord, because I felt the past gushing like blood from an open wound. I wept, my Lord, because my hate was gone, and I felt as if my sister lay there looking at me. Murder still lurked in my heart, yet there was a new bond of love.

I told her the agonies of those dreadful years. I told her of the living skeletons that stared at the sky and how they still stared at the sky when they were dead. My Lord, I lay with her in such sadness of heart. Amidst tears she said to me: 'I am your love, your sister, your undefiled one; come, come to me, and together we shall create a new world over the ashes of the past and the present.' The charge that I bring before you, my Lord, is this love, this overwhelming, tremendous love. Can it be, my Lords? Can it be?

When I lie awake on my solitary bed and listen to the faint rumble of distant trains in the long, dark, frightening night, I ask myself: Are we the first to bridge this awesome abyss through the wonder of love? Or are we insane, because it cannot be done? Perhaps history is more powerful, and so is our heritage. My Lord, you showed me the cross, and she showed me the cross, and I know that there must be an end to pain. In this age, when man can soar to the stars, the crucifixion must stop at last. My father once said to me: 'How good it is for a man to speak up!', yet, are words sufficient in an age that still reeks of gas chambers and charred flesh?

In the middle of the night, my Lord, I often hear voices from another world. My dead ones come alive and point accusing fingers. They threaten and demand that I kill my love. In vain. Every night becomes a long procession of the dead, bearing the words of that other world: 'The time has not yet come; you were born into a bastard age.'

Their lives were so tragic, and their words burn my nights to cinders, and I ask myself: am I a traitor to my people and faith, or else, am I the new man, who marks the end of a dying age?

I do not know. I need love so desperately. I beg you to tell me where I stand."

The candle has gone out; the night too is dying. There is not much time left before the new day begins.

The old Judge lit the third candle in front of him and said:

"I have raised this cross, my son, to show that everyone who suffers is part of the cross. Elizabeth and you are part of the cross, thus you are bound together eternally. Jew and Christian alike, who suffer with a meaning and who make meaning out of suffering are all brothers under the Father Above."

"I affirm your right to love this woman, yet not to bind her to you as your wife. What you have found, once your hate collapsed, was a suffering person, just like you and I. I affirm that the world must grow. Understand that hatred must die as this last candle died now right in front of your eyes, flickering to its end. The world is young. Not all men can hope to attain the growth you both gained during that night. The world would poison your happiness because the world is not of the cross. The Attorney says: let them part and go their separate ways. The Defender says: let them live side by side like brother and sister under the eternal roof of heaven. And I say to you, and this is my final word: the happy ending is yet to come."

The place was now in complete darkness. With a last, agonizing burst of brightness the candle flared up, then died. Outside a grey dawn was beginning to break; the smell of distant fields wafted in through the windows. Jonathan looked towards the Judges. In the tentative daylight he could only see their fading silhouettes. He thought: "I know this place, I have been here before." When? Before what? Was it now or then? The trial had swept away his conflict as though a huge river in flood. Now he knew that the new day outside meant the end of the old. He knew also that something within man must die, when he gives life to new things.

"My Lords," he bowed towards the empty seats, "Good morning to you."

But there was no one there any more.

44

Well, the real life story from which I derived my fictitious characters did in fact have a happy ending. And happily, it is not at an end yet. It happened in 1958. A middle-aged man married a German girl, who converted to Judaism. Now, thirty-three years later, the woman is herself middle-aged and the man is an old man. And yet, their relationship has grown into one of the happiest marriages that I have ever known.

What is important for you and me (and especially for me) to understand is, that I myself was at that time a young man. Elisabeth, the German girl in the story, belonged to my own generation Even then I was struggling to free myself from internal prejudices.

Today, there is a new generation on the scene. And I feel very, very differently towards this generation. Today, even from the start, there would be very little hesitation, few questions or dilemmas or conflicts. Certainly there would be no need for any trial, not even a trial by conscience.

You see here the problem that exists. And as I continue to build a picture of Judaism and the world for you, I hope you will come to understand ever more clearly the significance of such conflicts, the significance of the creative potential that arises from them.

You might ask, "How come that immediately after describing the symbolic significance of circumcision you speak of a man's relationship with a woman, a Jew's relationship with a German?" Well, without that you would be bound to miss some of the deep emotional implications of what I am trying to convey. The trial, the test, the testing of man as to the measure of his manhood and humanness are all interwoven with the development of Judaism.

The trial of Jonathan Rulph is a symbolic expression of the struggle against hatred and blame and persecution, of man's fundamental desire to achieve love and thus prevail. At the end of his trial Jonathan Rulph achieves peace and victory. Because when at the very end he looks around, the judges are not there any more. Without testing and trial there can be no peace, no victory, not even love.

Likewise too in the Book of Job, in the Old Testament. Job, a pious and upright man, was tried by God. I would very much like you to examine the testing and trial of Job in the original context, in the Bible.

The story of Jonathan Rulph was taken from the lives of real people who were eventually able to establish a bond and truly love each other. In The Book of Job you will find again and again, in a nutshell, the whole catastrophe and victory, death and resurrection of the Jewish people.

I have taken characters from the Old Testament and put them in a modern setting, writing my own version of the Book of Job in the hope that it will convey to you the essence of Judaism.

In this letter of mine I want to put before you not merely the facts, but the essence; and that essence is the love of man. During this process of achieving love - and it does not come overnight -, there are trials and turmoil. The Jew even argues with God, challenges God.

In the Jewish religion there is no devil as such, only what is termed 'yetzer ha-ra', the evil inclination. Unlike the Christian concept of the devil, which is in opposition to God, the 'yetzer ha-ra' (like its counter part 'yetzer ha-tov', the good inclination) is a servant of God. It serves the Almighty's purposes.

Please bear with me, and listen to this updated version – my own modern version – of the Book of Job. I have tried to express in it the true concept of Judaism as I see it. The characters and names are those in the original Biblical work.

THE BOOK OF JOB (1961)

1.

There was a man in the land of Men
Who was upright and perfect,
And feared no evil because he
Knew no evil. And he loved his God.

He was rich in day, in sheep, in
Spirit, and had everything that
Man desires: sons and daughters,
A loving wife and faithful friends.

2.

The sun shone upon him and taught
Him words that are secret words
Known only to the sun and the moon
And the stars, and the great empty space
Taught him the secret of the far Beyond.

3.

The flower of the field sang beauty
Into his eyes, and the valley and mountains
Of the vast land spread pleasure into his veins,
Pleasure greater than hides in the
Oasis of women.

4.

Now one night when silence fell like snow
And the sun lay faint beyond the cold mountains
And the mountains trembled naked beyond the fields
And no flower sent more beauty to his eyes:

That night as he lay awake and listened
To the uncanny silence of the Dark
Satan came to him and spoke across

The black velvet of the night.

5.
And Satan spoke in words that were easy
To his ears: "Job, my friend, do you recognize my
voice?
And Job whispered not to wake his wife
From her innocent deep dreams:
"I don't know you, Stranger,
I don't know who you are."

And Satan laughed and said to him aloud:
"I have lived in your heart and you
Deny your heart. I have lived in your bones
And you deny your bones.
I have lived in your dreams:
Do you deny your dreams, my faithful friend?"

"I am eternal like the fear you have not known
Because you have denied me, Job.
I am deep like the heavens and the seas.
I am your faithful friend and you do not
Recognize me, Job?

Without me there is no beginning
And there can be no end and no between,
Without me you cannot be Man
And cannot understand what the stars and the sun
The infinite space, the flowers, valleys and mountains
Tell you all …"

And Job replied, "I saw only good and God,
I have never seen you before."

6.
The night grew heavy and phantoms grew.
While Satan spoke it was easy still

To feel peace, beauty and virtue,
Good and God.
But it came to pass that Satan
Withdrew from the dark
And now he spoke from the darkness
Of Job's heart:

"I am not a mirage and am not a ghost
Now I am not a dream but I am you,
And now you cannot dismiss me any more
With your godly humble words."

Now Job prayed to God and said,
"Lord of my Fathers, help me to be free
From the whirlpool of my heart,
Help me to find my peace in You, my Lord.
O tell me now that Satan does not live
In my world, but only there in the outer world."

And God in His mercy talked to Job
And the words were easy to his ears:
"How have you grown rich in days
If you have denied my servant
Who speaks to you?
How can you understand me now?
How have you loved me then
If you deny the evil in your heart?
Weak is the man who denies the dark
Wishing only to see the light."

7.
Now Job cried and the salty tears did not
Wash Satan away:
"Why the pain, the desire of the flesh
Why can I not grow old in grace,
Why did I not die in the womb
Before I came out of the belly?

49

A thousand why's of wife, of aim,
Of night and day, of sleep, of breath,
Of life and death, and knowledge of the kind
That tears the bones apart from heart?
Why the boils, the wounds, the murders
And the rapes, and why You, God, if you allow
My living death?"

8.
(Pain grows into pleasure, pleasure grows into love,
And love grows into hate
And hate into the infinite
Depth of the night
And yet there is no relief ...)

9.
Then time has stopped
Satan stopped the earth spinning into space,
And stopped the planets dancing around the
Sun, and stopped the tears that flowed like
Rivulets.

And when everything was silenced and without
Life ... when everything had died an eternal
Death and only men remained alone
In the arms of the damp fear,
Job cried the curse of Man.

"Father Who aren't in heaven, cursed be Thy name,
Cursed be the hour when Man has turned his face
Towards an illusion of his heart.
Cursed be the hour when Man created You
Out of dust, out of sweat, blood and dirt.
Damned be the man who sings to You
Writes poems to you
Makes statues or paints pictures

For the sake of your Name.
O damned be the world! The grand illusion
Has come to an end.

10.
His wife, hearing these ugly words, awoke
In alarm.
"You be damned for the weakness of your heart
I married you young and strong, fearing God
And the Law, and now you are old and weak
Vulgar, sensual, and cursed.
Your youth has gone, because your
Faith has gone
Your wealth has gone
Because you have destroyed your wealth."

And Job cried into the night
"Why do you turn against me woman in my
Hour of despair?
Why aren't
You offering me drink
Of your love
To soothe my pain?
Why do you curse me
When I curse the world?
Why can't you bear my pain?

"Aren't you me, woman?
Aren't you the split image of man
Who was created on the first day of spring?
Aren't you me who wants to find the truth,
And unite with God in peace, in love, in death?"

11.
Hearing these words he spoke
His wife turned her back on him
And cried,

"Don't listen to him, my Lord
For his words are those of the snake
Don't believe him God
Because Your name is cursed on his wicked lips.
I am not him,
I am me
And without sin."

12.
So there in the darkness lay
A man and a woman created for unity
Of body and soul and there was
The empty space of timeless pain
Between the two.
And all this happened on that night
Because Satan appeared to Job
And he did not appear to his wife.

13.
Then neighbors heard the stormy
Words, and friends heard them too,
Because bad news travels fast
Amongst the sons of man.
And they came to Job and spoke to him
In the early hours of that tragic dawn.
Eliphaz spoke at first,
"I have known you Job
Since we played in the fields,
Many more summers ago than I can say
And we ran together under the big oak trees
And we shared more secrets than I can name …
Now Job, why have you turned
Against your father, mother,
Your wife and children, against
The Order, the Law, against (O forgive my words O
Lord)
Against your God?

Can you not kill Satan in your heart
By the mighty strength that I have known
In your heart and arms?
Can you not kick him, suffocate him,
Torture him to death, until he falls back into
The devilish rat-hole where he abides?
Here are we all your friends to help
In this saintly task;
Here is your home, your wife,
Your sons, your daughters,
And the Law. Can we not help?"

14.
Then Job answered Eliphaz and said,
"You are not my friend to say these words
I hear.
You are not the child I played with when
The trees stood still in the fields.
You cannot be my friend and deny
Him who exists in your heart,
Deny Satan who rules the
World with a sword ..."

15.
Then Eliphaz stood and turned towards
The waking Sun, and cried,
"This man is evil, rotten to the core,
Only rotten men see evil in their friends.
I deny the long years of love for him.
I deny him, my Lord,
And swear to You that I am sinless in my heart."

16.
When Bildad spoke, the Sun was rising
In the sky:
"How long will your anger last, O Job,

My brother and friend, my son and companion?
You see how your pain hurts my heart,
How your cries cut into my veins.

I bring you peace through the words
Of our Lord. Turn to Him, and your dark
Hour will be gone like clouds disappear
From the distant sky.
Pray to him for mercy, forgiveness,
For peace of mind, for love you lost."

17.
And Job turned against Bildad and said,
"Your words are empty shells
As my words were empty shells,
If I knelt on the earth and cried,
'Forgive me, Lord, I have sinned against Thee'
These words would not ring true to my heart
When Satan speaks these words.
My pain is thus: I cannot say
The words, because pious words to me
Are now but empty shells."

18.
Now Bildad thought he was a good man
And a true man of the Lord
And while his heart flamed with anger
Yet his words remained so calm:
"What else has Man but words
To share, to shape, to build, to plan?
Can words not be the cradle of the good,
Or else a coffin tightly sealed?
Are not the words that make
Man different from every other
Living thing on earth?"

19.

And Job replied, "My words of hate
Are better words than your words of love.
My words are filled with hate
And yours are but empty shells."

20.

So Bildad stood rigid like a statue of stone
And spoke many more words to Job.

21.

Now Zophar disliked the stormy
Seas of emotion
So he said,
"Let me see now what this is all about.
You are mature in years and mature in thought
My friend, O Job, a friend indeed.
You have lived your life obeying the Law,
Obeying the words and teaching others of
Those Words.
Until last night.
What is one night against so many thousand nights,
What is one bad dream against so many good dreams,
What is one curse against ten thousand prayers?
A man does not become a beast overnight,
A dog does not become a cat when the Sun
disappears,
The Sun does not become the Moon when the stars
Shine brightly in the sky.
Surely it is no crime to suffer wounds
And it is no sin to be sick at heart.
As the wounds of the flesh heal when
Time permits, so the wounds of the heart
Will heal in time."

22.

And Job turned against Zophar and cried aloud,

"Can one night not become an eternal night?
Can the Sun not become Moon when
Man is in pain, or dog a cat? Is not
The very curse on my lips the howl
Of the wolf, the growl of the dog,
Is not my very hate the beast in man?"

23.
Then Zophar thought for a long time
And said,
"Because what you say does not make
Sense to me, therefore you are senseless, Job."

24.
Then Elihu spoke to Job and said,
"Say more, my Master. I sense Wisdom
In your words."

25.
Now Job was taken aback with surprise and
Asked, "Wisdom? You say, wisdom in
These words of hate?"

Then Elihu said to Job:
"Master, the greatest truth is in pain.
I should know as I am crippled in my heart.
Your curse, O Master, does not attack the Lord
It only hurts earthly man who runs away
From pain. The Satan in your words
Is God's words in reverse,
Your very doubt pays in the same coin of faith.
Only the strong may see Evil in his heart,
The weak knows none because he's ruled by it."

Now as the clouds withdrew from the sky
And the infinite blue showed its naked heart
Job felt warm and opened wide his arms

To embrace this man who shared his pains with him.
And it came to pass that he sensed
The throbbing of Elihu's blood
And saw his tears and sensed the love of Man.
And the love of Man, he knew, was the love of God
And the love of Woman is the love of God
And the love of the world will be the love of God.

And no more words were said by any man
Because they only saw the two embracing in the sun
But they did not hear that God spoke to all
They only saw the tears.

26.
But the two stood there and raised their heads aloft
And only they heard the Voice of God.

27.
The others went home shaking their heads.

Now if you ask me what Judaism means to me, what I have distilled throughout my lifetime as well as my ancestors' lifetime from the many sacred and beautiful books of Jewish literature down the ages, I reply, "Hear O Israel, the Lord our God, the Lord is One." And then: "The love of Man is the love of God."

Two thousand years ago *Rabbi Hillel* said, *"If I am not for myself, who will be for me? And if I am for myself alone, what am I? And if not now, when?"*

Later on it was *Maimonides* who set himself the task of surveying and formulating the essence of Judaism. In his book titled *"Guide to the Perplexed"* he addressed himself to Jews who were confused and unsure of what Judaism was all about. He crystallized, somewhere in the 12th century, a list of the basic articles of Jewish faith:

1) *I firmly believe that the Creator – blessed be His name! – is both Creator and Ruler of all created beings; that he alone has made, still makes, and will every make all the works of nature.*

2) *I firmly believe that the Creator – blessed be His name! – is One, and no unity is like His in any way, and that He alone is our God who was and is and shall ever be.*

3) *I firmly believe that the Creator – blessed be His name! – is not a body, and no material terms can apply to Him, and that there exists nothing that bears any similarity to Him.*

4) *I firmly believe that the Creator – blessed be His name! – was the first and will also be the last.*

5) *I firmly believe that the Creator – blessed be His name! – alone is worthy of worship, and that no other being is deserving of our worship.*

6) *I firmly believe that all the words of the Prophets are true.*

7) *I firmly believe that the prophecy of our Teacher Moses (peace be upon him!) was true, and that he was the chief of all prophets, both of those that preceded him and of those who followed him.*

8) *I firmly believe that the Law which we now possess is the same which has been given to our Teacher Moses (peace be upon him!).*

9) *I firmly believe that his Law will not be changed and that there will be no other Law – or dispensation – given by the Creator, blessed be His name!*

10) *I firmly believe that the Creator - blessed be His name! – knows all the actions and all the thoughts of men, as it is said, "He that fashions the heart of them all considers all their works." (Psalm 33, 15)*

11) I firmly believe that the Creator – blessed be He! – rewards those who keep His commandments and punishes those who break His commandments.
12) I firmly believe in the Messiah's coming: and although he may take his time, I daily await his coming.
13) I firmly believe that there will be a revival of the dead at a time which will please the Creator: blessed be His name and exalted be His Being for ever and ever!

When everything has run its due course, and man has extended his love to his fellow man, and men have stopped to hate and to wage war, then one day, on a fiery chariot, the *Messiah* will arrive. The *Messiah* is conceived of as a human being who will come to all mankind to redeem it.

The establishment of God's Kingdom is here on earth, not in heaven, as Christians would have it. It means an age when brotherhood, justice and peace will rule the world.

The *Prophet Isaiah* (2, 24) has expressed beautifully man's love for his fellow, the coming of the *Messiah*, the end to human conflict, and the kingdom of harmony which the *Messiah* will bring to all nations of the world. This is how he describes the *messianic age*:

"And it shall come to pass in the end of days
That the mountain of the Lord's House shall be established
As the top of the mountains
And shall be exalted above the hills
And all nations shall flow unto it
And many peoples shall come and say,
'Come, let us go up to the mountain of the Lord
To the House of the God of Jacob
And He will teach us of His ways
And we shall walk in His paths ...
For out of Zion shall go forth the Law

And word of the Lord from Jerusalem 91183 and He shall
judge between the nations
And decide for many peoples
And they shall beat their swords into plowshares
And their spears into pruning hooks.
Nation shall not lift up sword against nation
Neither shall they learn war any more."

Just as in my story about Jonathan Rulph, where after trial and conflict there came peace, or as in the story of Job, where out of immense pain and perplexity there emerged a feeling of brotherhood towards all men, here is the concept of the advent of the *Messiah*, a human figure, who will some day arrive from some mysterious dimension and help mankind to become truly human.

It is instructive to consider how the sages viewed the coming of the *Messiah*. In *"The Book of Jewish Knowledge" by Nathan Ausubel* (Crown, New York, 1964), *Ausubel* describes succinctly what kind of age will precede the *Messiah's* arrival.

"In picturesque idioms, the Jewish writers gave a name to the troubles and calamities that would descend upon man, beast, bird, fish and all other created things. They call these calamities "the birth pangs of the Messiah." They said blood would ooze from trees, the dead stones would cry out. There would be heard a terrible clash of swords by a myriad of warriors, who would be battling in the clouds. And behold, hearing all that, mankind would be affrighted."

If you contemplate now these various calamities of beast, bird and fish, if you look at the current destruction of the environment, of blood oozing from trees, of stones crying out, of the clashing swords of a myriad of warriors who battle among the clouds, does it not amount to a description of a war waged from space, the threat or actuality of a nuclear explosion? According to the prediction of our sages and

60

writers we seem to have already arrived at the *Messianic Age*. And all that can save man is the love of man - the love of man, which is the love of God.

CHAPTER IV

JESUS WAS A JEW

It is now time, high time, for me – for us – to tell you that Jesus, who spoke of love and of loving and of forgiving did not teach a new religion, but the basic concepts of Judaism, because Jesus was a Jew.

Before the 19th century, no such statements could have been uttered. In earlier periods any reference to Jesus' Jewish origins was totally forbidden. Interestingly enough, various nations (Greeks, Romans, and Spaniards) foisted an image of their own national character upon Jesus. So he was seen either dark skinned or pale skinned; dark haired or blond. What he in fact was: he was a Jew from the Land of Israel. Some say that even well into the nineteenth century it was still very dangerous to refer to Jesus as a Jew.

Apparently one day Beethoven witnessed a particular religious ceremony in which a procession passed down the street with the various Christian symbols on display, whereupon he made a remark to a friend concerning "all this splendor for a poor crucified Jew." He was overheard and had to clear himself of the charge of blasphemy – and this as recently as the last century.

Jesus was not only a Jew; he was a practicing Jew, who observed all the commandments laid down by Jewish law, religion and ethics. He taught little new. He did not depart from the Jewish religion and the Hebrew heritage. In the Gospel according to Mark (12, 28 – 31), when asked: "What is the main commandment?" Jesus answered, "The main commandment is: '*Hear O Israel, the Lord our God, the Lord is One; and you shall love the Lord your God with all your heart, and with all your soul, and with all your strength*'; this is the first commandment. And the second one is thus: '*Love your neighbor as yourself*'. No commandment is greater than these."

The utter rejection of hatred and envy and greed and lying, the approval of humility and love for one's fellow man, indeed all the ethics that Jesus taught, are without exception Jewish ideas that can be found in the literature of the Jews – in the Bible and other sacred writings – centuries before Jesus was born. It was the basic commandment of the Law of Moses, *"Love your neighbor as yourself"*, that Jesus taught from these sources.

Every night before I go to sleep, I say a prayer, which my father and grandfather and all my ancestors down the ages used to recite:

"Master of the World, I pardon every transgression and every wrong done to my person, to my property, to my honor, and to all that I have. Let no one be punished on my account."

At a time when mankind was in complete darkness, my people's teachers taught: "When you ask pardon for your sins, do you also forgive those who have sinned against you?"

In the *Ethics of the Fathers*, Rabbi Hillel says (1, 12) *"Be of the disciples of Aaron, loving peace and pursuing peace, loving mankind and bringing them near to the Torah."*

In a previous chapter, in my own version of the Book of Job, I said that the love of man is the love of God. This principle was established long before Jesus arrived on the scene of history. It was this basic principle that he taught and tried to convey to the pagan Gentiles, who subsequently distorted and misunderstood it, to this very day, - creating the age of Fascism, National Socialism, and the Holocaust.

One hundred years before Jesus' birth the twelve patriarchs said: *"Therefore love one another from the heart. If a man sins against you, cast forth the poison of hatred and speak peaceably to him. In your soul hold no guile; if he confesses and repents, forgive him, or else catching the poison from you, he might take to swearing and thus sin doubly."*

The famous Christian prayer about *"Our Father Who are in Heaven"* is rooted in *Pirkei Abot* (5, 23) which also speaks of *"Our Father Who is in Heaven"*. The very notion of a Heavenly Father is a profoundly Jewish concept and permeates the Prayer Book to this very day. May I cite from the Jewish Prayer Book, which I read as a child? I grew up with it through my adolescence, and today I still think of it and say it in my heart at times of difficulty. Let me quote it to you, my young German friend:

"O lead us not into the power of sin or of transgression or of scorn. May it be Your Will, O Lord, my God and God of my Fathers, to keep me far this day and every day from arrogant men and from arrogance."

And then: *"Our Father, Who is in Heaven, show mercy towards us for the sake of Your great name whereby we are called. Fulfill unto us, O Lord our God, what has been written: At that time I will bring you in and at that time I will gather you."*

This means the Kingdom of God. However, the Church distorted this Jewish message of loving humanity.

Jesus was a Jew. He never claimed to be anything else. It was certainly not his intention that I, descendant of his blood and soul, should be told as a child by young Christian hooligans that I have crucified him and that I and my people should be killed just for being Jews.

It was autumn; dust blew in the wind. The wind came from the direction of Krakow. Over Auschwitz clouds gathered, and there was a smell of rain in the air. I stood there looking towards the wasteland where periodically the wind swept up the dust and moved it away into nowhere. The dust. The dust that had been people. The burnt limbs of six million men, women and children.

The autumn sky was stormy. I looked around; there was not a soul about and I felt my solitude and loneliness as never before. There were tears in my eyes as I looked at the swirling dust in the wind. Tears.

Then there was this man standing beside me. O, he was not very old, in his early thirties perhaps. He had dark eyes and dark hair and a tall forehead, and he just stood there. As I looked at him he too was weeping.

"My name", he said, "is Yehoshua. I know what you feel, because I too went through all that" and he pointed a finger towards the swirling dust and the lowering sky.

"Yehoshua", he said, "is my name."

So there we were, the two of us, silently weeping for our dead.

Memories came. The arrival of a transport from my hometown in July 1944: one group went to the left and was never seen again, and the dust is their dust too. Yes, they were burnt in the ovens. Members of my family, my friends, and so many others known or unknown to me. The rest, like me, went to the right. Some of us, not many though, were still alive. I turned to Yehoshua and asked, "Were you there too?" And he nodded and said, "Yes, I was."

There was now a bond between us, between this strangely dressed man and myself. Those of us, who were there and survived, share an invisible and unbreakable comradeship for the rest of our lives.

I asked: "Yehoshua, my brother, how did you survive?"

For some time he did not answer, and when he did, he was serious and his eyes looked towards the east.

"By the will of God," he said, "by His will, I have survived."

O yes, that made sense. During that fateful year of 1944 each moment of every day I too felt that it was by the will of some extraordinary power that I survived. The bullets, the beatings, the "selections" could all so easily have been my lot too.

"So", I said, "we both survived."

Again he nodded.

Now the storm grew stronger. The wind blew the dust into our eyes, our faces, our mouths. We shuddered.

He said: "This wasteland is so dead. No flowers, no trees, no grass, nothing green, no birds. Not even birds."

And I thought of the fields beyond the park where I had so often played as a child, and of the fountains which through some miracle sprang from the earth. The sun played in beautiful colors on the stream, and I thought of the girl, the first one I loved.

"Yehoshua", I said, "this is a dead land. Let's go."

He looked at me, his eyes piercing through my body, and said, "You know, one ought to stay a while. Just a while. To remember."

I shared with him some of my memories of this horrible place called Auschwitz. I also told him about my youth, and the colors of the field, and the slow rhythm of my town as it went about its business day by day. And the peace that I had felt as a child, and then the gathering storm. And the anguish that I felt because of the mysteries that hovered like phantoms around me. And then the return. The return after this hideous place when nobody that I loved was around any more.

He nodded and said: "Yes, I know. I know."

Suddenly I cried out: "Why?"

I looked into his young face and said to him: "You can't be more than thirty years old or so. How come that you say you were here? At the time of the Holocaust you were not even born yet."

A sad, sad smile appeared on his face as he said: "Oh yes, I was born all right. I was born a very, very long time ago."

An uncanny feeling flowed through me for a moment as I considered the apparent impossibility. How could this apparently young man have gone through all that I have endured?

He said: "I went through all this in Jerusalem."

"Jerusalem?" I asked. "How come?"

"It was not the Nazis, not the Germans then, you see", he said. "The Romans came to devastate the land. The Romans. Yes, it was their turn to conquer then."

"The Romans?"

"Yes, they set out to conquer the world. Just as *they*", - he pointed to where once the crematoria had stood, - "just as *the y* thought they would conquer."

"The Romans."

He went on: "Titus came, son of Vespasian. He conquered our land, your land, the land of your fathers, your ancestors. They conquered it, you know. And the king turned traitor as kings so often do."

He said it without hatred. "And others tried to save their skins, just like during this last war here ... well, some of them did, anyway. You see, people are people. Some", his eyes went sad, "became traitors. In those days it was still possible to buy one's life by betrayal. Here", again he pointed towards the barracks and the gathering swirl of dust, - 'here it was not possible." He continued: "You see, Jancsi," –he knew my name! – "you see, those were strange times. Do you remember when you were in the ghetto in your home town?"

"Of course I remember," I said, "I shall never forget."

"Do you remember how hopeless people were, how frightened?"

"Yes," I said, "of course I remember."

"And do you remember how the rabbis tried to put spirit into the dead souls of men and women by recounting the past and by recalling God's will and commandments and laws?"

"Yes," I said. "so they did. They did indeed."

"So," Yehoshua said, "I am one of those who in those turbulent years in Jerusalem tried to do the same. I tried to save the soul of a nation, when the nation itself was dying.

I said: "When was that?"

"A long, long time ago," Yehoshua said. "A long, long time ago. And they did to me just what they did to you and to your people here. Did I say '*your* people'? *My* people."

When I turned round and gazed at this vision before me, this apparition of Yehoshua the Jew, in a flash it crossed my mind: Could this be the man? Could this be he who, - my father had said -, was being killed every day? Could this man, this handsome young Jew, be the one of whom my grandmother refused to speak? Could this be the man in whose name all that evil was perpetrated through the last two thousand years?

As if he had caught my thought he said: "Yes. In my name they did that. I did nothing but teach the precepts and concepts and traditions of our ancient laws. And they did *that*. They did it in *my* name. But," he went on, "neither you nor I are responsible for what people do in our names. I did not come to sow enmity. I did not come to establish new institutions and organizations. What I tried to do was to teach, just as your rabbis tried to teach you in the ghetto of your home town. Men still must learn to grow and to return to the Source where everything begins."

"Once upon a time, "he said, "there arose a wind in the desert. But the dust it blew was not the remnants of the dead, but just grains of sand. And there a cluster of tribes, feeling abandoned and alone, looked up to the sky and saw the stars and the moon shining so near. Nowhere in the world, Jancsi, is the sky so near to man as in Israel."

"I noticed that," I said, "when I visited there twice."

"You see," Yehoshua went on, "when a man stands alone and afraid in the desert night with nothing but dust and wind all around, and he looks up into the sky, something strange, something very strange happens then. He looks into himself and into the infinite, and he sees the stars up there and the dark immensity of space, and asks, 'What is all this? Who is there? Who am I? Where am I?'

And with the questions, the answers too begin to come. Because, you see, there can be no answers unless and until somebody asks questions. Those tribes in the desert did ask, 'Where am I? What am I? What is this vast beautiful dark

68

expanse above and those stars sparkling like little diamonds?'"

"You see," he went on, wiping the human dust off his face, "that is how it all began. The rest came later: Abraham, Isaac and Jacob. And then, later still, our prophets, who heard the still small voice in the night, the still small voice that comes to man, when he asks these questions. Sometimes it comes to man when he does not ask. We are all children of the cosmos. Like the stars, you know, we too are parts of the cosmos, of the universe, of the system of a million, million universes.

"And then came the men to whom the still small voice appeared in the night. *Elijah* heard it and *Amos* and *Jeremiah* and *Isaiah* and *Micah* and *Hosea* and *Ezekiel*, all the prophets of Israel who heard the still small voice in the night. They were called upon by God to deliver *messages* to men. But it all started in the dust of the desert. Not under a stormy sky like this, that carries the remnants of human ashes. It came long, long, long before.

And then I appeared. At a time of foreign occupation I came to articulate to people the ideas and thoughts of all who came before me, all who had heard the still small voice. And they nailed me on a cross on a Friday afternoon. Only you can understand the unbelievable agony of this, my brother, - you, who were in this place. And the others, who died; and those who carried their tormented bodies somewhere else in the world: they too understand.

The church did not understand. No, over the centuries, the church never did. With perhaps a few exceptions, the Popes did not understand, over those hundreds of years. I did not come to establish a new faith, but to give hope to my own people; so that even though brutal forces destroyed the land, the human spirit would live on within man.

"Yet what I tried to do failed. Because you and I are here now in Auschwitz, years and years after the horror, still rubbing the human dust out of our ears and eyes and mouths and nostrils. It will linger there for a long, long time to come.

No power of wind can ever sweep it away altogether. No power will erase from human memory what happened here, my brother."

Now he was silent. It was my turn to remember that Jesus' Hebrew name was Yehoshua; I now remembered that, when he appeared to me at Auschwitz, I was in the autumn of my life, but he was merely thirty-three; and that he had died on the cross at the hands of enemies and traitors. But his spirit, the spirit of the ancestors whose values he taught, is still around, and nothing will ever kill it.

There we stood together, this young Jew and I, weeping over our dead and trying to shape (I at any rate was trying to shape) an image of the future, a much happier life. The Jew Jesus, Yehoshua, and I wept over our dead and felt very close. Very, very close indeed.

THE DEAD ONES (1941)
Translated from the original Hungarian by Rabbi Dr. André Ungar

It is a lie that they who Sun-gaze, eyes afever,
And seek some miracle in all things, are alive!
I saw them, flesh and blood, these all-exploring dead.
At sunset I saw them as they spied the soaring rays
Yet no tears filled their eyes, their heart did not exult
Heavenward.
On the seashore I saw the dead: their souls
Proof to the rippling miracle of waves, just dumbly
stared ...
O Lord, my Lord! ... Praise be to Thee who gave me
life
And life to Man within me, that I am not of the dead
whose
Heart can no more throb, and in whose heart never
awakens
Thy Name!
That I am no pulsing dead, O Lord
Praise be to Thee!

WE GO ON (1942)
Translated from the original Hungarian by Rabbi Dr. André Ungar

It's naught … we plod along the path
An endless sea the sky above,
The wonder-sky enchants our soul
It's naught … We must away. Enough.

Our cheeks are rusted by the sun,
Fire-floods in our blood race,
Jeering curses trail our steps,
It's naught … On tramps a deathless race.

Can you see? The ruffians glare,
Stones fly hissing, slanders bray:
Let not the slander halt the march,
It's naught … we must be on our way.

Do your parched lips long for kisses?
Your blood rebels like glowing coal?
Well, let the blood burn, scorch the body,
It's naught … One day we'll reach the goal.

Does sweet remembrance amble in you?
Beckons an old sea, ancient lane?
Childhood landscape, dusty dreams –
It's naught … Go on, ignore the pain.

Go on if you would reach the sun,
Go on, your heart tough choked in tear,
Your heart will find peace in the earth,
It's naught … For it is God you bear.

PART TWO

FINDING MEANING IN LIFE, DEATH AND HATE

I

So far I have been talking to you about the meaning of Judaism and about the persecutions – and in some strange ways the two are connected.

In my view we have been persecuted as a people, as a nation and as a religion because we have conceived the idea of an invisible God, Creator of heaven and earth.

We have been persecuted because this concept and its ethics are to this very day still almost wholly alien to mankind, even though lip-service has been duly paid to them.

We have been persecuted because the Jewish idea and Judaism itself are still unacceptable to people. Recent events as well as the history of the last two millennia demonstrate this very clearly.

I mentioned earlier that in Jerusalem there sat a great assembly called the Sanhedrin, the Council of Elders. It had seventy members. Whether this was a primarily political institution along the lines of a Parliament or else exclusively concerned with religious matters and laws, is still an open question. There may well have been two distinct legal institutions, dealing with two different aspects of the same subject.

Mosaic Law envisaged such a gathering of seventy elders; this has been practiced until Roman occupation put an end to it.

At a time when mankind was stumbling in total darkness in Europe and elsewhere, living practically like animals still, in Jerusalem a Supreme Court held sessions, enacting law and creating order out of chaos.

Some of those laws concerned social justice. Others dealt with procedural matters such as the summoning of witnesses, the inadmissibility of hearsay as evidence, and so forth. This kind of parliamentary democracy was practiced both in Israel and Judea a long, long time ago, and reached the West much later.

From what I have been saying thus far and from the recollection of my personal experiences, surely my pride in my people's history, ethics and values must be quite obvious.

To some measure I have recalled the pain and suffering, and tried to convey this to you, hard as it is to do. Those who have never been persecuted cannot fully understand what it feels like. Those never threatened with indiscriminate murder (murder motivated purely by hatred for one's ideals and beliefs) cannot understand what it feels like to adhere to these ideals even at the peril of death.

We have survived throughout the centuries, reduced in numbers, yet we are still committed to our ideas, carrying the sacred scrolls both in our hands and in our hearts. This is the destiny of a people that will not give in and will not give up.

Persecution however was never as great a danger to the Jewish people as assimilation was, and is. There is far more risk of our disappearance in times of toleration than in times of intolerance. A persecuted group develops a kind of defense mechanism. You build a wall around yourself. The enemy may pierce through and hurt you, he may even break through the wall from time to time, he might even kill you within the walls. But those who remain will build other walls. The more pressure you put on a Jew, the more he remains a Jew.

My purpose here is not to indulge in propaganda for either my people or my religion. We are not a faith that seeks converts, in fact we discourage proselytism. Conversion is left to the initiative of others. If somebody wants to become a Jew, great obstacles are put in his or her way. But if the candidate for conversion is sincere, knowledgeable and persistent, we accept him and his descendants for ever. From there on there is no difference between born Jew and convert; a Jew is a Jew. So it is not recruiting propaganda that I am

74

hoping to put before you, but rather one survivor's experience of his own religion, people and ethics, a system that has been misunderstood for a very, very long time.

What I also want to put to you is, however, not simply what we have been and what we have done, or what we feel and think, or what our history and laws are, but how all this affected this one particular survivor, myself. This is not the cry in the night of a defeated people over lost battles and wars. We have never been finally defeated; not so far. And I believe we shall never be defeated, either. *After all, in the history of the world there has never yet been a nation reborn from the ashes of persecution and exile after two thousand years, until we Jews recreated the State of Israel, a democracy, in its original place.*

What I want to put before you are not only the tears, the humiliation and pain, which are part and parcel of our heritage, but also the net worth, the philosophy and poetry of it all. If this were an attempt to present Judaism to Gentiles, others – far more knowledgeable – could do a far better job by presenting a systematic account in all its aspects. I have not covered even a tiny fraction of the subject. My concern was to focus on what I consider to be of relevance to you.

What follows now is something of a personal story, although it is perhaps a collective one as well:

Here is a man, a middle-aged man, who had learned at an early age that he was different from others. He did not choose to be different. He is so, simply because others say that he is. The impact of parents, teachers and others of the external world on his mind and soul was tremendous.

I believe that the very experience of pain is the spur for the renewal of energy.

As the years passed, it became ever clearer to me that the negative is the potential for the positive. Frustrations in life and in living are the potential for satisfaction. My total human experience, my experiences as a Jew and particularly as a

75

survivor of the Holocaust resulted in a new philosophy and in an almost poetic vision about life, people and the world.

This philosophy, which grew out of my experiences, underscores the strength which comes out of weakness. What are its essential features and components? How is it possible that a middle-aged man, somewhere along the road to resurrection, finds contact within himself, with ideas, thoughts, feelings and poetry, with *messages*, that come from the depth of his being? How is it that instead of utter and total defeat, there is a revival of body and soul?

You see, I have grieved over the loss of my loved ones. When I returned to my native Hungary, - where none of my dead were buried -, the ghosts of the dead still haunted me. The first task was to bury them within myself. Burying the dead is important for the living. When I realized this, I symbolically buried them with the ancient rituals of my faith, reciting for them the millennial *Kaddish* prayer for the dead. I had no time to do so before. I had so many to mourn: father, sister, brother-in-law, their child, uncles, aunts, and so on. For each one of them I had to say a prayer. It took me a long and painful time. Each day I buried one of my dead. My mother is the only one who lies in Hungarian soil and was buried properly. The rest of my family disappeared – possibly in that smoke and dust which still linger around Auschwitz, as I told you in my vision with Yehoshua.

For days at a time I kept their faces and movements and words before my mind, learning to say goodbye to them through memories and tears, many tears, and through the ancient prayer of the *Kaddish* which connected me to my origins.

Then the process was over. The past was gone. The fear was gone. I began to feel love moving within me again, moving my muscles and my nerves and my whole being, as it ought to. Then I was free once more to turn to the woman I loved, to give myself, to create new life. I have two children now. They are just about your age.

I don't know when and I don't know how, but it was then, after the burial, that the still small voice mentioned in the Bible began to gain some personal significance for me. Please don't misunderstand me. I do not hear voices, not in the sense that the mentally ill do.

I have so many questions about life, living and dying that one day, in the stillness and solitude of the night I began to ask questions about our existence. And when I formulated my questions clearly, then from within, out of my own experience, answers began to come. What the Sages of Israel had taught me helped me to ask my questions and I began to receive some answers.

I want to share with you some of these questions and answers. Not chronologically, descriptively or scientifically (as I would in my world and in my work), but in the way that I have experienced them. I want to hand it over to you and perhaps through you to others of your age and generation, with this *message*:

If you can formulate your questions and structure them clearly, the answers will be forthcoming from the computer of human experience ... a computer with a soul. This part of the book, this part of my letter to you, is therefore a symbolic journey from questions to answers, which I want to impart to you. This is the other side of the darkness, where light shines above the horizon.

Near the end of the agonizing period, while I was burying my dead, I once had a dream. Let me tell you of this dream before we proceed any further.

I was standing near a wall. It seemed like the Berlin Wall, which separated East from West. This wall in my dream, however, was not in Berlin, but in some unspecified place. On my side of the wall where I stood, the sky was grey and a desolate desert surrounded me. No trees, no grass, no flowers, nothing: A state of complete rejection. I felt alone, without any contact with anyone. And there was this wall, this huge wall, in front of me. Yet I knew that if only I could glimpse at

77

what was on the other side of the wall, the picture would be quite different.

With enormous effort I clambered up, just enough to be able to look over. The world I saw on the other side was one of ineffable beauty. Never in my life had I seen colors so alive. The afternoon sun shone with brilliance. It was Jerusalem. Not the Jerusalem I have heard of or seen in pictures or experienced in person, beautiful though it was. What I saw was another Jerusalem. There was life; trees swayed in the wind, bursting with green, buds and flowers. And the smell of citrus trees. Impossible to describe. People were moving about their business. There was peace in God's city. And there in the window facing me was my grandmother, of whom I have spoken before. There she sat and beckoned me towards her as if to say, "Jancsi, come, come!"

Desperately I tried to pull myself further up, so as to be able to climb over the wall. I longed to reach what seemed like paradise to me. Then I woke up. I did not know whether I was capable of getting to the other side or not.

… Almost like Moses, who was given the chance to gaze into the Promised Land but, did not make it.

For months and years afterwards I kept wondering: have I in fact crossed that wall in my dream?

Now to my answer: You be my witness and judge whether I did get there or not.

My ancestors, images of men who were near and dear to me, and great men whom I admired, one day seemed to have merged into a composite figure that appeared before me. This figure was neither the Prophet *Ezekiel*, nor *Moses*, nor *Joshua*, nor *Jeremiah*. It was an old Jew, a very, very old Jew, who began to give answers to my questions.

Come, share this journey with me, one of the most important journeys of my life!

II

From the summit I looked down into the valley whence I came and where I have lived for a long time. It seemed as if the valley, with all its memories, lay in a completely different dimension, and now my task was to bring up my experiences from the valley below to this mountain and thus at last make some sense out of them.

Across the passing years I have had so many questions down there, but somehow I could never receive answers; there was always such a hurry down there in the valley. Moments, hours, weeks, months were all glued together like putty; I could hear no responses to my questions, no *messages* came amidst life's rushing winds. I had lived, but seldom experienced the sense of life. There was some pleasure, much conflict and pain, failure, sometimes success. Time rushed by and then congealed and became a monstrosity of extraordinary dimensions. I felt this great weight of time and I was afraid.

I stood there amongst the peaks enveloped by the peace and silence of that moment. I knew that at last I would gain answers to many of the questions that lay - like barren women unable to bring forth life - somewhere down in the valley. I had to bring these questions, their vast multitude, to this place, where there was no competition, no struggle for survival, no enemy, no blood, only the wind and the strange elation of the altitude.

Down below I had often questioned whether I existed at all. Now my lungs were filled with the freshness of new air under an open sky, and I heard myself shouting: "I am!" The wind carried my voice over the peaks and brought back the answer: "I am."

Then something strange happened. A new voice unfolded within and asked amidst the rushing wind, "Who are you? What are you?"

I knew that there were rules. I had to open my life's pages, only then would I receive answers. So many times even before my great journey began, did I sense that I had to bring forth my questions, formulate them clearly, and then I would find the truth.

I knew that the man was very old, that he possessed the wisdom of the ages. But I never dared to imagine how old he really was.

He sat there under an old tree that must have stood there for centuries. He sat there cross-legged like a Buddha. As I moved closer I could see him more clearly. He was not a priest or monk of any kind; rather, he looked very much like one of the '*mussulmen*' of the concentration camps I had seen so many, many years ago. Men, who had given up all hope and were beckoning for death to come. Yet this man was very much alive, so much so that in his presence I wondered if I myself have ever known the kind of vitality that radiated from him. Covered in a blanket of some sort, he looked very small and insignificant. Yet his eyes beamed with youth and life and a kind of strength I had never seen or encountered before.

Accustomed to life in the valley, I thought I was imagining things; this old man must surely be dead. Yes, they killed him, just as they have killed millions in those ovens. But he moved, beckoning me to him, and smiled the smile of a young man.

I said to myself: "This man is beyond death. Thousands of times they have tried to kill him, and they failed. He walked out of wars, defeats, inquisitions, pogroms, gas chambers. Yet here he was. Alive.

Further down at his right I saw a village. Smoke was rising from distant chimneys. Music wafted in the wind and it seemed as if singing too was heard, coming and going in waves. Or was it prayer? I moved quite close to him and sat on the sun baked warm earth and again I thought, "How is it that I know this man? Where have I seen him before?"

80

A peaceful silence lay between us for a very long time. I could not ask anything because, frankly, nothing occurred to me.

Noticing my confusion he smiled and asked: "Do you know what day it is today?"

I swayed my head in denial. He said: "It is the seventh of July 1944."

No, it couldn't be, I said to myself. It could not be. The old man was wrong. Decades wrong. Why, here we are now in the 80ies and 90ies.

"Yes," he said, "it is the seventh of July, 1944."

Down below, where a minute earlier a peaceful village had been dosing in the sun, I now saw electrified barbed wires and barracks and the chimneys of the crematoria. I saw thousands of men and women crawling like animals; I heard dogs barking and Kapos walking with whips in their hands. I saw black-uniformed SS-men. And I saw myself down there, a young man with a shaven head in the uniform of a slave.

"I don't understand," I stammered. "I … I … I ca – came here to find peace after all these years … and you plunge me back into the … the worst hours of my life."

"How can you find peace if you deny your worst hours?" he said very quietly, almost apologetically.

"I have struggled for so many years to bury my dead. What are you doing to me, awakening the past again?"

After a while he said: "You have buried your dead. And you have made something of your life. But have you absorbed and digested the past, made sense of it? What does July 1944 mean to you one generation later?"

"What does it mean?" I asked, "I haven't given any thought to it." I felt anger rising in me.

"Well, isn't the purpose of our meeting precisely that you at last learn to make sense of it all?"

III

"Tell me then: how can you understand all the hatred that surrounded me as I was growing up into manhood? There are so many things in my lifetime that I still cannot comprehend. God's face too has changed; it seems no longer as innocent as it did during my childhood. I don't know what kept my love, my capacity to love alive. All around me the world is still going through convulsions today. Millions of people are still being killed. The Holocaust is not over yet. It seems that mankind has learned little if anything from the events of July 7th, 1944, the day of my arrival in Auschwitz. Old man, you say that I cannot find peace if I deny my worst hours. Can one never say: 'Enough! I want to bury the past and get on with living?'"

And he said: "You cannot get on with living with all that confusion within you."

"All right then," I said, "Tell me: do you understand it? Do you understand all that has happened?"

"Yes, I do," he said.

IV

"Be aware of feelings that you cannot find within you. You spoke of hatred surrounding you. Tell me: are you yourself free of hating? Does hatred belong only to your persecutors, not to you?

After Auschwitz was over, you felt ill; you were ill for a long, long time. I watched your second Auschwitz slowly looming on your horizon. You were depressed and anxious, afraid of places and of people. You felt pain in many parts of your body and your mind. What do you think has created all that sickness?

You say, '*they* did'. In a sense of course you are right. But have you ever examined your own heart? Are you yourself capable of hatred? And do you still deny your hatred? You see, your own innocence stands in your way and blocks your path.

You were a victim. Victims are receivers, not dispensers of pain. But when after the war your second Auschwitz came, what else but your own hatred gave you all that pain? You almost killed yourself with it. And if your hatred could potentially kill you, could it not also – under certain circumstances – kill someone else?

Now you may think that what I am saying is warped; that when looking back on the Holocaust, issues such as the personal hatred felt by the victims are irrelevant … You may also feel – and in this you may be right to a certain degree – that it is sacrilege to say such things which might be construed as condoning the actions of the Nazis.

Let us simplify issues.

For centuries the Church has taught people to hate the Jews. The Nazis took over and carried out the unconscious desire of the Christian world. All I am now saying is that the victims too harbor hatred. But by and large they can only turn that hatred against themselves.

Now if you can accept this hatred which appears to be innate in all men, does it then not become a quirk of history that you are the target of the blows? I must tell you this very clearly because if you wash your hands of hating, you will never understand what has happened to you and your people. Did I say '*your* people'? … *Our* people.

Once you can accept your own hatred, you will begin to understand the Holocaust. Believe me. An understanding of our world cannot come from displaying our wounds ad infinitum. The moment must come when you admit that the hatred which destroys is your own hatred too. What happens to an individual or to a people that can never express their hatred? You must ask yourself that question.

If hate – innate, inborn hate – is not expressed, only two alternatives are left open: Self-destruction, or some kind of extraordinary, creative existence. Our people, the Jews, have dealt with our hatred unlike most other nations in human history. We turned it into a search for truth, and have given the world many great people in the process. The process itself means this: we, as the Chosen People (for whatever purpose we have been chosen), are not free from hatred, but have learnt to use it in a constructive manner. Perhaps we have had no other choice. Yes, we have given great men to the world, but perhaps our greatest gift to humanity could be the lesson that there can be other ways of expressing hatred than killing. We know this, not because we are superhuman, but because we were compelled to turn our disadvantages into assets down the stormy centuries. There was simply no other way.

So you see, the Jew's hatred of his Gentile persecutor was ultimately transformed into the service of, and I daresay the love of mankind. We are the people of the Law. Why do you think God chose us, not only as the butt of blows but also the recipient of values and attitudes for which it is worthwhile to live and die? We were chosen to be persecuted in order that our internal world may be turned upside down.

The Red Indians however, were not able to turn their hatred into love of humanity. They destroyed themselves because they had not learned to use their hatred in another way. Unlike the Jews, they had no written laws to guide them during their persecutions to help them learn resilience.

Now once you have been able to recognize your hatred for what it is and to make something creative and new out of it, then, you know, you can love too. You said, 'I do not know what kept my love and my ability to love alive.' Let me tell you, it was the skillful use of your hate (though you may not have been fully conscious of it) that has kept alive your love. Loving and hating do not come from two different sources. The source is the same. Both, if expressed in a creative way, come from a source of creativity. Or, I might say, from the Creator Himself.

The message we must carry to the world is that feelings, good or bad, are feelings, and we must not be afraid of them.

If we are, we deny our humanity and in the process we become, like the Nazis, inhuman. We must profess the *message* that the impossible is possible; that love and hate, if used aright, are brothers; and that there are ways in which people can learn to be creative rather than destructive and murderous.

Jancsi, you cannot bury the past. It is your only source of creativity."

V

"You say that the Holocaust came about because the Germans could not use their hatred in the right way. What are you really saying? My family is gone, my friends are dead, a precious world of what was my home in Hungary has perished. And you talk about the creative use of pain and hate? Do you really think I care about the reasons for Nazism? As I look down into this valley of agony and death, could anything explain or justify those happenings down there? Do you think that your philosophy will put at ease those who are marching to their deaths today, tomorrow?"

And he said: "Those who are dead are dead, and you are alive. The living must crystallize some meaning out of death. Just as there can be no love without hate, so there can be no life without death either. You may ignore the truth about living and dying, yet even if your ears are deaf, that truth is still valid. The *messages* that I am bringing to you will have far reaching implications for you, for your future, for the generations that will come after you. Shall the ultimate *message* of the Holocaust be nothing more than a tortured people's unavailing cry into the night? Don't you think that you have survived in order to tell more than merely a tale of death to your children, to a new generation of Germans, to a new and perhaps sublimely beautiful century?

Our world is no longer sure that life is good. Since the war values have changed. Many former taboos have been lifted, yet people are no happier and life is no better. You must tell this generation, and the next, about things that are eternally unchanging, despite Auschwitz; despite Hiroshima and the rest. You can be a *messenger* if you allow yourself to be that."

"What *message* shall I carry?" I asked, "the word of a dead God?"

"A dead God," he answered patiently, "may communicate as many *messages* as a living one. And who, if I might ask, decides the birth and death of God? You? Your pain?"

VI

"Have you ever considered this? Only a *spark* is needed for life to begin, to flow, to grow, to change into forms of being. So a child is born, bearing this spark in him, and he dies in the ovens of Auschwitz. A child is dead. Yes, that child has died; died a cruel death. Yet it is not the final end of his existence; the spark is eternal. Does the fact that the child died as a human being necessarily mean the extinction of its existence? It appears to me that what we call human life is but one form among many possible forms. What if those who died a cruel death have perhaps taken a different route to living? Would then the face of God change from a dead God into a living one again?"

VII

"There are connections between feelings that are each other's opposites: between life and what we call death; between everything that exists on this planet and what is beyond it. You and the Universe are connected by invisible wires. You are part of everything that is alive and dead. You are the carrier of great, unknown secrets, and therefore a part of you can never die. Only outward forms change. Essentially, once life began anywhere, at any time, it moves on and on into eternity. Eternity. If your God died down in the valley, then it could only have been a self-induced illusion to start with. Because everything that exists is a part of God, is God Himself. The form of your thought, its structure and volume represent only one wavelength out of many. Your existence as well as its limitations is rooted in the world, the cosmos, the universe. Those who died still live on, for example in the dimension of your memories as well as in the memory of other survivors.

Jancsi, after all those events down there, you must learn many things anew. Learn that God handed over to Man responsibility for his own life and for the kind of existence that will prevail on planet Earth. He cannot interfere with what you consider good and evil, because such concepts, just as love and hate, are of your own making. In this human form of yours you have needs. Those aspects of life which fulfill your needs are perceived as good, and those that frustrate you are bad. Likewise too with the concepts of good and evil. Yet they are your own creation. The positive and negative poles of electricity are neither good nor bad; they are simply positive and negative. But without such polarity no energy can be created. This is a law of nature. Yet those opposites exist within you because you have not yet learned to fulfill your destiny as a man. Millions are unfulfilled and therefore carry evil within themselves. You must learn that unhappiness is evil, whether caused by oneself or by others. Freedom means fulfillment; the opportunity to grow. Because you can grow."

VIII

"I am impressed by what you are saying. No disrespect is intended, but I have heard and read similar thoughts before. I know that your aim is to help me understand my world, my own life as well as other people's lives. Yet thus far I find it difficult to relate all this to my own existence. You speak of connectedness, yet I can see no connections among many events in my life. They seem to be isolated incidents without much significance. Before I can grasp the greater issues of Man's place in the universe I need to understand the meaning of my own life, how the events fit together. Is there really a unifying theme within and among the fragments of my life? I must tell you about these things before I can grapple with the kind of dimensions you are talking about. May I tell you about some of these fragments which I suspect might be significant yet somehow do not seem to add up? I know that I can learn a great deal from you; but please allow me to do it my own way. At times words alone do not seem to help.

Will you bear with me while I put before you odd bits and pieces of my life? With your help, I might then understand how it all hangs together."

IX

"During the summer of 1944 I made an attempt to escape from the camp at Troeglitz. But after a day the task appeared impossible, and I had to give myself up. I was given a terrible beating by the SS. After all these years the scars are still on my back along with a persistent rash..

Then one night Lily, my second wife, (Eva, my first, was killed in Auschwitz) touched my skin and said she did not like the look of that rash. Would I seek medical advice? Reluctantly I went to see some doctors. At first they were not unduly concerned. But Lily insisted, and I found an outstanding specialist who felt a large tumor reaching right back into my spine. An operation was performed. It turned out that I had cancer: a malignant growth that could have been the end of me.

There I lay in the hospital bed, unable to move. The pain was unbearable. The surgeon said that he had removed the growth, but whether it would recur would only be known years later.

I remember a night when I could not fall asleep. Memories assailed me; my bitterness had reached a furious crescendo. I was forty four years old; I had had a young wife and family who had gone through hell. Now, years after that inferno, the same hell caught up with us. I felt it terribly unfair that I should die of the injuries that I had received such a long time before. I resented the fact that through my tumor the Nazi beasts could enter England.

I told you that during the night memories assailed me while I was lying motionless on my bed. But what was so strange, you see, was that these memories were of ordinary events of life and living. None of the great scenes which, I should have thought were the really significant ones in my life.

As if frozen in a photograph, I saw my mother reaching into a basket and fishing out some old socks. Halfway through the gesture she halted and smiled at me sweetly. I myself must have been quite small, since the basket seemed enormous and she herself very huge. I saw a field in springtime; I was lying in the grass. The grass was moving around me like a living curtain, the sky was blue, and the birds, both as they landed and in mid-flight, were talking – yes, talking – to each other. Though I appeared to be alone, I knew that I was not, that the truly important things (the birds and the grass) were all around me and Mother somewhere not too far. Flies buzzed and butterflies fluttered. Yes, all that came back to me as I lay on my hospital bed.

And again, many years later, another night. My flesh and soul were burning with desire. Eva and I were sitting, holding hands, by the banks of the river Gyongyos. It was a beautiful night, the Moon shone like a jewel. Again, I was contented to be there with her, with the river, with the night. You see, on that critical night the great dramas of my life did not appear, only episodes of seemingly little significance in the ultimate order of things.

Those and many more such small events filled my night with tears. I was saddened by the thought that I might never again experience such ordinary things. It seemed to me then that the whole purpose of life was just this; events of no great significance, no great desire, no great achievement ... just the experience, the texture, the commonplace. I was sorry to leave life behind; not because of great burning desires, fulfilled or unfulfilled, but because of the simplicity of life itself. There and then it came to me: we are so caught up in the struggle for survival, we try so hard to drink from the cup of life that in the end we cannot swallow our mouthful.

Then the nurse came in. She was alarmed by my tears. I could not tell her what was going on within me. She concluded, not altogether mistakenly, that I was afraid. She said nothing. There are times when words lose their effectiveness. Gently she leaned over and kissed me. I was so moved by this beautiful though wholly unprofessional gesture that I felt a great calm descend upon me. She had entered my solitude and gave me hope with that kiss. Hope to look forward, not to any great future, but to the small, humble, precious normalities of life, despite the rather dim realities of that phase."

X

I expected that once more he would respond. Frankly, I was looking forward to yet another outpouring of great wisdom. I was not quite sure what I was waiting for, but it was certainly not someone, however wise, lecturing at me. I wanted real communication, some that went beyond mere words. As I said before, in connection with my nurse, at times words lose their efficacy.

90

Somehow he must have understood this. Still sitting there as before, he was now still and quiet. I was beginning to feel uncomfortable. Then all of a sudden I looked down towards my right where at first a peaceful village had slumbered in the sun and where then the horrors of Auschwitz had appeared - all these were gone. Now I saw … indeed, what did I see?

Some years earlier a former fellow-inmate of the camps brought to my attention another former victim who began to feel that the London Police were after him. He had no reason to feel like that, yet he did. Eventually he suspected that his apartment was bugged: *they* were after him; *they* were going to finish him off. The world had become a nightmare for him and his family as he constantly sought for precautions against hidden microphones. When I saw him he was willing to talk to me. Despite his madness he knew that I could not be one of *them.* He knew that I had been in the same camp as he, and roughly at the same time too. I knew that no words could help him dissolve this terrifying sense of persecution. In any case it was very difficult to converse with him since, lest *they* overhear him, he would only talk in whispers. I suggested to him that we put a contraption in his garage. He would hit a lever which in turn would hit a bell. But we placed the bell so far up that it was almost impossible for him to succeed. So we both kept hitting the lever with a big hammer. One day he managed to reach the bell. In fact he hit so hard that the energy he must have invested was enormous. Soon afterwards he began to speak normally. Before long he went back to work. His nightmare was over.

Now on my right hand side, down there, where a short while before I had seen the Auschwitz of July 7th, 1944, I saw him, this former comrade, standing in the sun. He was stretching and yawning and, generally speaking, he seemed to be perfectly happy with himself and his world.

Seeing this I turned to the old man and questioned him. Without any words he pointed towards the valley where my comrade was standing. I was shaken for some time by what I saw. My mother was there with her basket. She looked up at me, just as she had done on that fateful night while I lay on my hospital bed. I was five years old (I saw as if everything in a mirror) and was chasing butterflies. And Eva and I were there by the river Gyongyos. And he, my comrade with the lever and the bell and hammer whose devil I had exorcised, was also there. In fact he was at the centre of the stage! The nurse was there too and she leaned over me in the hospital bed and kissed me. Yes, everything that I had told him about was there *in action*. But that was not all. I saw the SS dragging me away after that beating with my bleeding back, and Lily was there in our bed in Mill Hill touching my back and saying that I ought to go and see a doctor. Everything was there, and *simultaneously*. What was so extraordinary about this scene was that there appeared to be some communication going on among the characters of the various scenes. For example, the nurse talked to me while I was a five-year-old and helped me chase butterflies. My comrade sat down with Eva and me beside the river and told us how happy he was that I managed to get the aggression out of him. Eva said something to the effect that I really could do such things because basically I was a poet. "You see, Bernard, he is basically a poet. Therefore he doesn't need to use words for things like that; he just does them."

There was a connectedness among everything and everyone in that scene.

I looked at the old man with amazement.

He just sat there as before and did not say a word. To be frank, I was so fascinated by what was going on that the old man himself began to lose the significance that I had originally attached to him. A nice old man, true; a friend whom I knew from somewhere … God only knows from where. That was all. What was important now was the experience of *connectedness* amidst the various stages, aspects, feelings, and thoughts that kept jumping forward and backward in my lifetime. And it was all so natural as if it could not possibly have been otherwise.

Once the flow of time was broken up and rearranged in a different pattern, everything began to make sense. As if there was another flow of time, from the future to the past. Or maybe it was all in the present. I don't know.

XI

As time passed, a close friendship developed between the Old Man and me. There was no need any more to be physically with him on the mountain top. Once I brought him down from the pedestal upon which I myself had placed him, I could call upon him anytime, anywhere, as long as I was alone with myself. I could get on with my life down in the valley, yet he was with me as a witness and, when I needed advice, as an advisor. He was always there. On the whole, he kept himself in the background and waited until I called upon him, usually at night before going to sleep, or during the day when I was tired and lay down and closed my eyes. Yes, all I had to do was close my eyes and imagine him there and then we were together on the sun baked earth, he sitting under that old tree and me facing him.

There were times when he felt compelled to communicate with me under different circumstances: Usually, when I was going about my businesses and was missing something important in my communication with people, he would gently point out this or that; and I was always very grateful to him because, as a result, my life began to be ever richer and fuller. He told me that I would experience a great deal of variety in my life; that I would travel to the far corners of the earth; and that I ought to carry a survivor's kit on truth to many people who also wanted to survive … to you too, my young German friend, to you.

This predictive aspect was new in our relationship. I was fascinated to find out that whatever the Old Man predicted invariably came true. Before my first contact with him I had thought that our connection would be a kind of one-shot deal

93

that I would be granted some great illumination, and then I would return to my world with peace of mind and increased wisdom. But now he became a part of my life down below in the valley.

No great revelation had taken place. Rather, the solitude and loneliness which I had carried within myself since July 1944 slowly came to an end. I was not alone any more, not for a single minute. This man of Auschwitz, or whoever he was, was with me all the time, practically day and night. And it was good.

XII

"Great Old Man, I must speak to you about belonging, or rather about not belonging. There is, I think, some instinct in man to claim some territory, some place for himself. Those who own land, however small, belong to that land. Some belong to their flats, their houses, their gardens, their plots. Others belong to groups, political parties, churches, and clubs.

You see, I have never belonged anywhere. And, as I come to think of it, this not-belonging has opened up new vistas on the world in my mind. (Or ... has removed barriers between the world and my mind.)

Oh, it was quite another matter than wanting to belong. Of course I did. As a child I wanted to belong to Hungary. But what it could offer me was at best a kind of nationalism or chauvinism that had to die in the end because it was sick. You see, I was excluded from that kind of belonging, and I am really glad that I was excluded. This is the main problem with belonging: it often works at the cost of excluding others. In time I learned that I *cannot belong*. Even if I wished it, longed for it, I could not belong ...

When you are young and other children play games and you are not allowed to participate, you are hurt and alone. "Mummy, they don't want me." But as you grow older and find that you are *nowhere* allowed to become a part, gradually you begin to experience an exhilarating kind of freedom. You see, if they had allowed me to belong, I could not embrace all the world, as I do today, or embrace you, my young German friend. Since I don't belong anywhere, I belong everywhere.

"Great Old Man, you spoke of opposites and how they fit into a whole. I am not suggesting that there isn't a trace of sadness in me for not being able to be a part of things, to belong to a majority. Of course there is. But without this separateness I could not fully be myself in the world today. My countrymen are not only Englishmen but also Bermudians and Hungarians and Scotsmen and Welshmen and Americans and Canadians and Israelis and Germans. Believe it or not, Germans too. When I go about my business in Edinburgh, London, Calgary, Las Vegas, San Francisco, Amsterdam, Saskatoon, Berlin or Jerusalem or wherever else, I am not a tourist. I am a survivor, selling a survival kit. So people open up and speak to me *as if* I belonged to them. No, perhaps I am wrong. If I did belong to them in the sense of 'belonging' as it is commonly understood, they would not speak to me so openly. At one time it hurt me to miss that cozy feeling of group togetherness which might have allowed my individuality to dissolve into others. I missed that; at times I still do. But with the passing years I have discovered that individuality could not be maintained if I *did* belong. To be *me*, I cannot, I must not belong.

Thus, what started as a sad historical affair back in my native land turned out to be an asset of great value. You see, had I belonged, you, Great Old Man, would not be at my side, and the young German – and Germans – to whom I so desperately want to speak would not be at my side either. I would have erected a barricade between me and him or her or them. I would have no need for you, Great Man. Nor would you need me because then I would be fulfilled by my group or groups. I would not have had the solitude or loneliness that led me to search for you.

Does a Jew want to belong? Oh yes, he does. The Hungarian Jews did their utmost to prove to the mad nationalists that they too were Hungarians. Without much success, they kept displaying their wounds to the Gentile world – wounds received during World War One. They showed decorations they had been awarded for bravery. To no avail. When the chips were down, brave or not, they were booted out.

I must say it is a splendid feeling to be able to enter a country without much fuss or interrogation. When I come home to England, I am always allowed to cross the threshold freely. 'Home to England' is what I said, Great Man. Yes, my home is there. My children were born there. I feel at home there. Yet I don't belong. An Englishman of Norwegian ancestry once said to me: 'You belong here *de jure* but not *de facto,* and that's the difference.' I suppose that sums it up neatly. It is not a question whether I want to belong or not. In fact I do not."

XIII

"Jancsi, you belong to the six million dead. You belong to all who are persecuted. You belong to a long tradition that gave laws to mankind in a lawless world. You may not belong to 'the old boys' network', but to a much, much older one.

Tell me: where does an Englishman belong who goes to bed hungry because he is old and sick?

Tell me: where does a Hungarian belong who has lost the cock-eyed world he had once lived in?

Tell me: where does a Bermudian belong who can find no work on his tiny island?

The kind of things you talk about are only the outward, superficial aspects of belonging. The real roots go much deeper. One does not belong to a language or to a geographic location but to all mankind. If man cannot belong to all men, he belongs nowhere."

PART THREE

THE GREAT OLD MAN OF AUSCHWITZ
TRANSCENDING TIME

I

At this point of time when the Great Old Man had become a part of my life, following me on my journey through life, breaking the ice of my aloneness, I often wondered who he really was. He knew so much about me; my whole life was an open book before him. It seemed as if even before we had met he had already known everything about me. In a sense he knew my past and my present and, I had a sneaky suspicion, my future too.

I wanted to find out. I did not want to have a one-sided relationship, with me as the talker and him as the advisor.

As I have told you, he wasn't just one person but a composite, a synthesis of many others. He came from some very deep recess of my mind or perhaps of existence itself. I believe that Carl Gustav Jung calls such figures *Archetypes*. I have given another name to him – or to them. I call him the *Paraphant*. The Greek term *'paraphasis'* means someone who talks to you and to whom you can talk. So the person (or persons) whom this particular old Jew represented became my *Paraphant*. More and more, I was able to have a dialogue, a two-way conversation with him. Thus far these conversations consisted of advice or words of wisdom given by him. Quite frankly, I was beginning to be a bit irritated. Of course, I did want the wisdom too, but I wanted to get to know him. When I have such an intimate relationship with someone, I must know, I must find out.

So one day in my bedroom in Mill Hill in London I turned to him and asked: "Tell me, Great Old Man, who are you?"

And he said: "You really don't want to have an answer. You are really after the experience, aren't you?"

I didn't quite understand. I said: "What do you mean, 'words and experience'?"

"Words are words. And experience is experience. When you looked down and saw the unity of time, the flow of time from present to past, from past to present, from future to present – that was not a word, or words. That was experience. And thus, instead of telling you who I am, or who we are (by now you have gathered that I am not one person but what you call the *Paraphant*), I shall help you gain the experience."

I whispered a polite 'thank you' and knew that it didn't mean very much, since I did not quite understand what he meant.

He went on: "Jancsi, be prepared for a surprise, even a shock. As soon as I allow you to face the experience itself, your time sense will be disoriented, the time dimension will have yet another direction."

Smiling he added: "But by now you are used to such things, aren't you?"

I still did not understand; I was still waiting for an answer to my question 'Who are you, Great Old Man?'

II

It was about ten o'clock; I knew it because the guard had told me so. He looked at the clear sky and at the brilliant stars shining above as we were standing there, and he said: "Yes, it's ten o'clock."

On the left there was a fire. People were in a state of confusion, running hither and thither and shouting. The fire was not that great yet, and they were trying to put it out. The Great Old Man was sitting in his room, his head bent over a scroll. As I entered he pointed politely, if somewhat impatiently towards a chair as if to say, 'Please, sit down.' I did. I felt that I ought not to disturb him in his study of the Torah or the Talmud. So I just sat there and kept quiet.

Suddenly he turned to me and said: "Jancsi, my boy, you do realize that they've started a fire?"

I said: "Yes, I noticed it as I was walking through. Is it serious?"

The High Priest turned to me and said: "Yes, it is serious."

And suddenly he called me by my Hebrew name, Mordecai ben Aharon. Then he repeated: "It is serious, Mordecai ben Aharon."

I don't know why, but it seemed perfectly natural that he should call me by my Hebrew name, although practically no one else ever did. Oh, I've been called by this name, but only when I was called up to the Torah on a Sabbath morning, first as an adolescent after my *bar mitzvah*, and later as an adult. It is always an honor to be called up. On the occasions that I attend synagogue, if the rabbi notices my presence in the congregation, he usually honors me by calling me up to the Torah, calling out in a loud voice: "Please step forward, Mordecai ben Aharon."

But this was a different situation. Somehow I was feeling, if not exactly dizzy, then light-headed. Yes, I might put it that way, light-headed.

"I intend to see how long it will take for this fire to prevail," he said. "I am afraid we must decide upon something very drastic."

"We?" I asked.

"Yes," the High Priest answered. "You see, this is the end."

Now he got up and was quite calm. "For the time being, this is the end of Israel."

I said: "The end of Israel? Forgive me, but the State has hardly been declared. Thirty years ago, in 1948, I heard on the radio that people were dancing in the streets of Tel Aviv when the State was established and *David Ben Gurion* became the first Prime Minister of Israel."

Again he was smiling. "Oh Mordecai, you are mixing up the time, as I expected you would. You see, I am talking about *now*. The date is" – he smiled, "oh, the date ... Well, which calendar do you want me to refer to? - The Jewish one or the Gentile one? Now according to the Gentile calendar this is the year 73 of what will be called the Christian era."

Almost in a whisper, he added: "Seventy three years ago the man whom *Pontius Pilate* crucified was born."

I felt that light-headedness again. For a while I just sat there looking at his face. Come to think of it, he was not that old. Still, quite a bit older than I; I appeared to be quite young.

I asked: "What must we do?"

"We must tell them. No, I will tell them. But you must be a witness – more than a witness – to the end."

I said: "Pardon me, Eleazar ben Yair, but what on earth are you talking about?"

"Mordecai, there comes a time when life as it is lived loses all significance. We have arrived at such a point in history now. This means", and once more he leaned over the scroll and repeated, "This means that there are times when the body must die in order for the soul to survive ... the soul of Israel."

"You mean..." I said.

"Yes, I mean that people must kill themselves or kill one another in order that they should survive," he said, "though suicide is taught to be against Jewish Law."

"But this is insane! How can anyone survive if you kill them?"

"Mordecai, I am speaking about survival. I am not speaking about life or death."

I had to find my orientation because that light-headedness was on me again. The little room we were sitting in was gently going round and round. In the flickering candle light the shadows grew long. Where have I seen such flickering candles before? Still, that was not important now. There we were. I had an eerie feeling that I was simultaneously present

101

in two dimensions. I was in a house in Mill Hill, with red buses passing by; I believe a number 53 bus was just careening past. From down below came my children's voices, I no longer know whether quarreling or laughing. Lily was saying something, perhaps shouting at the children over the voices of television. And here was this man saying to me, they must kill one another.

"Eleazar," I said, "I find it difficult to adapt myself to the situation here ..."

He smiled for a moment and said: "Well, I've warned you that you might find it difficult. And as you want to get to know me – and us – better, you will find it increasingly difficult, you know."

All right, I am used to difficulties, I said to myself. But I had so many questions. I asked him again, "Eleazar ben Yair, would you please tell me what my own role is in all this? Where do I fit in?"

"Mordecai ben Aharon, you were always a part of it, never mind that you also have another dimension. Never mind that with one ear you hear the police car and the sirens in Deans Lane in Edgware in 1958. There is always a duality of dimensions. Here and now, on this fortress of Masada, you are witnessing one of the great historical events of your people. Let me go further and say, you are not merely a visitor, you are in it with us here."

A cold terror ran through me when he said this as I realized the implications of his words. I would have to die with them, so that one day I might live in England with my wife and children.

Now I realized what moment this was and where I was. I also realized why the guard did not look at his watch but at the constellation of the stars when he told me it was ten o'clock. I was sad and frightened, but I was proud, yes proud, too.

"I must ask you some questions before the terrible tragedy happens. Would you spend a few minutes with me? I know that very soon you must speak to the crowd and prepare them for the inevitable, yet would you be willing to tell me a few things first? I want to write them down and share them with people, with my readers, with the world."

"Yes," he said, "I will give you a few minutes."

"It may sound unimportant to you, but during the last few years I have been working with unemployed people on an island called Britain. They were unemployed because of the war and the injuries they had suffered. Forgive me for asking you at this extraordinary moment, indeed it may seem inappropriate, yet tell me: am I on the right track? Am I doing the right thing? Can this, what's happening here at Masada at around seven minutes past ten in the evening shed some light on my problems?"

He thought for a while, turning the pages of an ancient book, and said:

"Do you know how old this book is?"

"Of course, it goes back to Babylonian times."

'No, no," he said, "I mean this particular book. This book is three hundred and fifty years old."

"So?" I said.

"Well, it says in this book, in this particular book which is three hundred and fifty years old, that man cannot live without work. He must work, not simply to keep busy or to make a living, but to give sense to his life through the meaning of work itself."

"Okay," I said, "that is what the book says. But before the tragedy engulfs you, and perhaps me, and the people, and we all die, tell me this: in the Britain of the 1950's, am I on the right track? Does what is happening here today have any bearing upon the work I am doing with the unemployed in London, in the Borough of Hendon?"

And he said: "Yes, Mordecai, it has a very important bearing."

He thought for a while, the High Priest of Israel. Then he came quite near and looking at me he said: "You do realize, don't you, that 997 men, women and children have found refuge here from the conquering Romans?"

I said: "Yes, of course I know that."

"We have come here because down in the valley of Jerusalem everything that was near and dear to us was destroyed. And man cannot live without the symbols of the past and the deep-rooted symbols of his faith."

"And what has this to do with the unemployed in Hendon?" I asked.

"As far as I can understand it," and he looked towards the west as if trying to see my life and work in 20th century London, "you are doing a bit of rebuilding, aren't you? You are restoring, or at least trying to restore, people to a meaningful life who are considered work-shy or unemployable. And you are doing it, Mordecai, after an extraordinary conflagration in the world known, I gather, under the name of World War Two.

We here, at the other end of history, must destroy ourselves in order that eventually we can become free again. You referred to 1948, when the State of Israel was reborn. Well, if we do not kill ourselves now, you will not be able to work with the unemployed in London and carry our spirit into your work.

You are right; my time is running out. What is it that you are really trying to do with those people, most of them Gentiles? Surely you are trying to reawaken their spirit so that once again they can embrace their wives with pleasure in the night, so that they can walk the streets of London with a spring in their step, so that they can go about doing whatever they do joyfully and with contentment in a free country. Without our death, you know, you could not even begin to think of this vocation."

I said to him: "High Priest, you speak about freedom. Are you saying that the drama of Masada is relevant to minor matters, such as my own life and work? Are you telling me that without our dying here on this mountain before the conquering Romans enter this fortress, my own work could not take place?"

And he answered: "Please understand something. No work of man that aims to bring freedom to, or inspire a sense of freedom within others, can take place without a precedent. Let me just sum up this situation and then relate it to what you call your insignificant work in England ...

We have lived as free men in this land, trying to make laws that conformed to the will and instructions of God. Since we are human, we have failed in many, many ways. We had political parties that not only opposed each other, but actually fought each other. We, God's own people, have become no better and no worse than any other nation in this part of the world. The only thing, it seems, that can bind us together, is a common enemy which threatens our existence, our institutions and our traditions. A state came into existence upon the land that had been promised to Moses, upon the land where Abraham stood and built an altar to sacrifice his only son. The promise was fulfilled, and we became obsessed with, oh, what men are always obsessed with: possessions, greed, stupidity.

Then the Babylonians came and destroyed Jerusalem and carried us into exile, which lasted a very, very long time. By the rivers of Babylon we sat and wept, vowing that if only we could once again return to our own land, we would be different. But it was not so. When we did return and rebuilt the State for a second time, we, like any other people, repeated the same mistakes. And so now Rome has come, under the Emperor Vespasian and his son Titus. And down there in the valley is the General Flavius Silva. In a sense they are but the instruments of God, sent here to do once again what we need: to be herded together into one people, since we are not developed enough to do what we must do of our own free will. So we shall be destroyed again. And we shall be reborn again after the sacrifice that we bring here in the name of freedom. We are not going to be slaves. No woman here will open her body to a Roman as a slave; no man here will accept the yoke of Rome and work in Rome as a slave. No child here will be brought up to worship idols. You see, Mordecai, to die for freedom is to create it.

Now as for what you call your insignificant work, not only will you die here tonight, but you will die again and again down the centuries at the hand of kings and popes and other conquerors, including the great Northern barbarians known as *Germani*. Not for the first time nor for the last do you face this fire which, - just look - , is now burning in Masada. The Romans have finally managed to set on fire the last remnant of our heritage. As I look into the future, I see the flames of the crematoria, and I see you looking into those flames. And after that fire will have been extinguished, you will live. You will take your tortured body and mind to a land that will give you a chance to be restored. Just like the ants: as soon as you destroy their world, they create and rebuild another. And so it should be. Now no man can hope to be able to do more than put a single brick into the building of freedom. Whether this brick goes towards the building or rebuilding of the Temple in Jerusalem or of an English city in the 20th century is immaterial.

Helping disillusioned, broken people who had fought for freedom to find the meaning of freedom in their lives again, be they Jews or Gentiles, is the whole purpose of life and death.

Thus it is in our spirit that you do the work that you will do after you die a hundred times and live a hundred times. No memorial will enshrine your name. We do not need memorials. You see, memorials can be destroyed overnight. What remains is the work itself.

Now, Mordecai ben Aharon, I must go and address my people and prepare them for death and for eternal life. And when, after the mass suicide on this mountain top, you find yourself back in your home with your wife and children, amidst the red buses running in the streets and the police sirens rushing after criminals, remember this: Everything can be destroyed except that which comes from the heart and is expressed with the heart. Your writings may endure longer than any building. You see, even our own Temple has been destroyed, and now for the second time. Temples can be destroyed, but ideas that are written down can never be destroyed. There comes a generation that will not merely read those words, but live by them. One day, when the Messiah comes, the written words and all the feelings that had inspired those words will bring about the Kingdom of God. Then Israel will have accomplished its mission and will merge into the cosmos, into the universe from which all ideas and feelings come. That is all I can say for now."

I trembled as I heard these words uttered on this fatal, tragic night. I walked away and left him there facing east.

As I walked past the guard, he said: "This fire cannot be put out any more."

And I said: "We shall have to die."

Down in the valley Flavius Silva and the Roman legion were preparing for the final assault. And I opened my eyes in my bedroom in Mill Hill and went downstairs and put both my children on my lap and watched television for a while. Then I said: "Time to go to bed; your have to go to school tomorrow."

All this happened simultaneously, within the great relativity of time and space.

III

I had asked the Man of Auschwitz, 'Who are you?' And indeed, instead of words I received an experience beyond words. I ought to tell you that in fact my work in those days was with the unemployed in London. I was trying to help people see themselves as if in a mirror. But it was not weaknesses, but rather strengths that we were seeking in the mirror. From all the experiences that I have undergone so far,

I have come to the conclusion that man's strength lies in his weakness. That the proper question is not what is wrong with man, but what is right with him, and that the rightness lies in the wrong.

IV

Time knows no frontiers, and neither does human experience. Therefore you are continually witnessing interplay between my personal past and the past in general; between the collective past of my people and that of mankind as a whole on the one hand, and the present and the future on the other. In order to introduce to you the nature, philosophy and practice of my work, I will move in different dimensions. Without these different dimensions, I believe, human life is devoid of real color.

V

Let me talk to you about an ancestor of mine, a man called Claudius Marcellus. He lived in Rome just about the time when the Romans conquered our land. At that time he was a grown man already.

I feel it is of some relevance that I share with you some of his life as told to me by my Paraphant, the composite figure of the Man of Auschwitz, when I asked him, 'Who are you?'

Claudius Marcellus was born in the year 20 AC in Rome, the capital city of the world at that time. His father was a Senator of Rome, a close friend and advisor of the Emperor. Brought up as a Roman nobleman, at one time he served in the Praetorian Guard, the rarest and highest military honor available to a Roman. The Guard was responsible for the personal safety of the Emperor Vespasian. Claudius Marcellus' mother came from a rich merchant family in Alexandria. Her own father was a dealer in silk from the East who eventually found his way to Rome. Claudius lived the

108

life of the rich. A private teacher from Athens taught him philosophy, mathematics and geography, all the subjects that a fashionable young Roman had to know at that time. As a child he played in the vast garden of the villa at Caesarea. The garden led down to the sea where he built sand castles and staged battles. His friends were the sons of other noblemen.

The sun of Italia tanned his skin deeply, and as the women of Rome would later on say to one another, he was a very handsome young man.

As I said already, he did his military service as one of the Emperor's guards. In his spare time, just like others, he drank and slept with many girls, slave girls as well as daughters of the Roman nobility. By the age of twenty he had come to the conclusion that this kind of life somehow failed to satisfy him to the same degree that it seemed to satisfy his comrades.

When he was twenty six years old, he asked his father, the Senator, whether he could arrange a posting for him in his mother's home town, Alexandria in Egypt. After some time he was indeed commissioned to oversee a building program that the State had undertaken just outside that city. When he arrived there, at first he again just mixed with the aristocracy. His life in Alexandria was basically no different than it had been in Rome. He continued with the drinking parties and with women of various shapes and colors.

After some three or four months there, a vast depression began to engulf him. The physicians in Alexandria gave him herbs and extracts from poisonous snakes and other medical substances. These appeared to alleviate his misery somewhat. But deep down in his soul he was empty. He longed for peace of mind that so far had eluded him.

The physician who treated him was a Greek named *Artepanus*. He had long talks with his patient, telling him about a man crucified in Jerusalem some years earlier, and about the values and concepts of a religion and nation known as Hebrews, whose land was occupied by Rome. He also informed Claudius that near Alexandria there was a sect known as the *Therapeutae* (the Greek term meaning physicians or healers – possibly healers of themselves) who were spiritual heirs to those Hebrew teachings.

Claudius ventured forth to look for these people, and he found them on a hill overlooking *Lake Mareotis*, just south of Alexandria. For a young man, brought up on the idea that Rome could not be wrong, that the Emperor was infallible, to discover a totally different kind of philosophy and outlook, that for him was simply world-shattering.

This Jewish monastic order consisted of men and women whose ancestors had established it long before the birth of Yehoshua / Jesus. They considered the outside world, be it Judea or Egypt, to be decadent, sick and violent, and they chose to reject and resent every kind of cruelty and cynicism. They repudiated the institution of slavery, claiming the ancient doctrines of the Hebrew Bible and Sages which proclaimed that man was born free. If any man was sold into slavery, he had to be freed within seven years. Even seven years were deemed too long a time, because God created man equal and there were to be neither slaves nor slave owners.

Remember that while in 19th century America slavery was still a lawful institution, in Alexandria, as far back as almost two thousand years ago, slavery was not accepted. Quite possibly the Hebrew concept of abolishing slavery has been around for some four thousand years.

Now Claudius Marcellus began to see clearly that Rome could be wrong and that the Emperor was not infallible. At that very moment he also realized and had to admit to himself that at heart he had become a traitor to Rome and to the so-called ideals that Rome stood for. The *Therapeutae* also believed that the ultimate healing came from within, that the source of true health was inside man himself, and that no person could cure another but only help him in the process of curing himself.

Claudius Marcellus recognized within his own soul the truth of this statement. He fasted with the others, he was taught to pray and to meditate deeply, he gave up (as did the others) all earthly possessions, he worked very hard, he rested on the Sabbath. He ate only vegetarian food, abstained from alcohol and foods injurious to human body and soul. He promised to remain chaste to preserve his physical and spiritual energies.

His soul responded and began to blossom into a flower of unutterable beauty, to his own benefit as well as for all around him.

Although he was already in his twenty eighth year, he offered his body for circumcision so as to identify himself with these people who, he felt, saw the light of God much more clearly than Rome ever had.

After a hard day's work he would study the Torah and the other sacred books under teachers of exceptional sensitivity who searched for the inner meaning of life and living. He now felt he had found true meaning in his life, and he wanted to learn as much as possible about healing, so that one day he might return to Rome and heal others according to these teachings.

When he spoke to his teachers about Rome, they, the Rabbis, insisted that he must not seek converts, that he must under no circumstances try to persuade others that he was right and they were wrong, that man must ultimately find the answers within himself, and that no external pressure or persuasion should ever be brought to bear upon pagans or barbarians or others. He was only to learn and master the art of healing, so that he might open up or at least help to open up the healing process within others.

Conversion would take place by example, not through words. The Rabbi said to him: "If people love you and can feel your love for them, they will want to discover their own love. And with that love the road to God starts."

On Sabbaths he participated in the choir which chanted thanksgiving and glorification to God. Men sat on one side of the synagogue, women on the other. Sometimes they sang separately and sometimes their voices merged as if in the most intimate union known to men and women, yet their bodies were kept apart. He was taught that differences of color, race, culture and even religion were unacceptable in the eyes of God. God sees only people, whatever their origin, and man is born free. And within that freedom lies the possibility of healing.

He was taught that any society or culture which discriminates against any other society or culture is sick, and that man must liberate his own soul in order to overcome the sickness of the world around him.

Sometimes at night, as the stars and the moon shone brightly above, they enacted secret rites and rituals in order to bring peace into the troubled world.

Claudius Marcellus, whose name was now changed to Abraham, learned and absorbed into his soul the mood, the beauty, the sanctity and the ideals of this people. One day he asked the leaders for permission to return to Rome. "Stay here," they said, "the world out there is not ready for you, if it will ever be." But he argued: "I want to take back these concepts and ideas because Rome needs them, and without them it will be destroyed."

The answer came: "Rome will be destroyed because anyone who lives by the sword will perish by the sword. And anyone who lives by God will be raised into eternity by God."

In the end, however, the leaders of the Therapeutae agreed, and Claudius Marcellus went back to Rome.

His father, who was aging and in frail health, grew very angry at such outlandish ideas such as the possibility that weakness can be turned into strength. He also could not accept that his son should mix with what he regarded as rebels and bandits who aimed at destroying Rome. Abraham Claudius begged to be allowed to help his father recover from his chronic illness, but he was repudiated.

About eighteen months after his son's return from Alexandria the old man died. Claudius' father was buried according to the ceremonies and practices of Rome and his wife and son mourned.

After his father's death, a remarkable conversation took place between Abraham Claudius and his mother.

One night she came into her son's room where he was studying sacred Jewish tomes. For a while the old lady just stood there and listened to her son's Hebrew chant. Abraham Claudius did not even notice her presence for some time. Suddenly he turned round and saw her and wanted to stop. She said: "My son, you are a *Rofeh*. – (the Hebrew word for healer). In great surprise Abraham looked up and asked his mother: "How do you know this word?" Tears now appeared in the old lady's eyes. She answered very simply: "I know because I was born a Jew." She stood there, her tears pouring down her cheeks; he sat, his left hand still on the holy book, unable to speak. And when at last he regained the strength to speak, he asked: "You, Mother, ...you ... a Jew?"

Again she answered very simply: "Yes, I was born a Jew. And in case you don't know it, you too are a Jew; you were born a Jew, according to our laws."

"Why didn't you ... ?"

The old lady raised her hand and said: "I promised your father that I would not reveal this as long as he was alive." Then she went on: "Oh, there is nothing to be ashamed of. There are prominent Jews here in Rome. But you see, we", then she changed it, "they, the Romans, fought against Judah and Israel. Your father did not want them to know that I, who came from Alexandria, belonged to a people that fought against Rome."

The young man stood up and embraced his aged mother. He too was weeping. Now mother and son stood there having found each other fully for the first time. When the tempest and turmoil of emotions at last abated, she quoted from the Book of Exodus (15, 26) "For I am the Lord Who heals you".

Understanding what she meant, he said quietly: "I know, Mother, that I am but an instrument in His hands. I know that all healing comes from Him." "Then," his mother said: "You will be a great healer, a very great healer!" And for the first

113

time, she called him by his Hebrew name: "A great healer, Abraham."

"Man was first created as a single individual in order to teach the lesson that whoever destroys one life, is considered by the Torah as if he had destroyed the whole world, and whoever saves one life is considered as if he had saved the whole human race." (The Talmud)

VI

Let me now move to the Middle Ages, to the year 1559, when the famous Jewish anatomist and surgeon, *Amatus Lusitanus,* wrote in his medical testament: *"I swear by the Eternal and by His most holy Ten Commandments ... that I had never, at any time, done anything in my treatments except what inviolate faith has handed down to posterity; that I have never feigned anything, or added anything, or changed anything for the sake of gain; that I have always striven after this one thing, namely that benefit may spread forth to mankind ... all men have been considered equal by me of whatever religion they were, whether Jews, Christians or Mohammedans."*

And *Arturo Castiglioni* (1874 – 1953) wrote in his "History of Medicine": *"What is particularly notable, and what makes the history of Jewish medicine more interesting perhaps than that of other people of antiquity, is that one can often observe that traditions and concepts have been absorbed and so to speak filtered through the moral and legislative system of Judaism, and what a decisive role has been exercised in this process of assimilation by the concept of Monotheism which ascribes to the Deity the power of healing. As a result of this concept, Hebrew medicine differs from that of all other people of antiquity."*

114

Abraham Claudius Marcellus practiced his arts of healing in Rome. His healing was based on the idea that men are but instruments in the hand of God, and that the healing comes from within man whom God had created in His own image. He became extremely popular and produced a number of remarkable 'cures' among the Romans. Indeed many of them felt that there was much more than simply a particular technique or skill involved in the practice of this most unusual man.

From the time he went to Alexandria until the age of fifty two Abraham Claudius Marcellus did not marry. He used all his energies, skills and faith for the treatment of the sick, particularly among the poor and the slaves of Rome. Among the slave population at that time there were a great number who originated from the Land of Israel. The authorities tolerated Abraham's ministrations to them only because they were unaware of his Jewish origin. He did not openly advertise that he was a Jew.

On April 15th of the year 73 AD, on the very day that he turned fifty three, he woke up at night in a sweat, filled with fear he had never known before. Almost automatically he reached out as if to find a partner of body and soul beside him. But there was no one there, and his heart felt empty. He felt incomplete and greatly disturbed by this incompleteness. He could not fall back to sleep all that night. He could neither understand nor explain the turmoil in his heart and soul.

Weeks later the news arrived that it was just around that hour that Masada had been burnt down and its defenders had taken their own lives.

Up until then Abraham Claudius did not concern himself with political issues at all. When the news came that the Jews had been defeated in the Land of Israel, that the last stronghold had fallen too, as those last 900 people cried the name of God and freedom into the wilderness of the world, he remembered his tortured night.

He knew then that he had to step out of the ivory tower of medicine and do something for his people. But he did not know what to do. From that night onwards, ever since he learnt that not only had the Second Temple been burnt, but Masada too had fallen into dust and ashes, he was greatly concerned for the preservation of the Torah and other holy books, lest they be lost for future generations.

His opportunity to do something came quite unexpectedly, seemingly as a coincidence. Next to the event of his journey to Alexandria, this 'coincidence' became the greatest turning point in his life.

Soon after he had heard the tragic news about Masada, one night members of the Praetorian Guard knocked on his door. Most respectfully the officer in charge said to Claudius Marcellus: "Sir, I have orders from the Emperor himself that you come with me at once."

"Is the Emperor ill?" asked Claudius. The captain of the Guard did not respond but merely repeated: "I have orders from the Emperor that you come immediately," adding, "and bring all necessary medical materials with you."

Lucillia had been the mistress of Titus, the Emperor of Rome, for some time, as a matter of fact ever since he gave up his Jewish mistress Berenice, who was the sister of the Jewish King Agrippa II.

On the night that Titus summoned Claudius, Lucillia had a nosebleed in the middle of the night. The court physician was unable to stop it. Lucillia panicked, and so did the Emperor, who hated the sight of blood.

When Claudius arrived, there was a commotion and turmoil that had to be dealt with first. With great respect he asked the Emperor and all others to leave the room. Then, without administering any drugs or rushing into any medical procedures, he calmly talked with Lucillia. Putting a pillow under her head and a handkerchief under her nose, he made her comfortable, and then said: "Tell me, what is really bothering you?"

Through the handkerchief, Lucillia said: "You know what is bothering me, Claudius Marcellus. My nosebleed is bothering me."

Very calmly he asked her again: "Lucillia, tell me what is bothering you," he added: "apart from your nosebleed."

It took some time for the dark-haired, pale, beautiful young woman to calm down. Then she began to weep. She cried for a long time uninterruptedly. Claudius did not stop her. When she had stopped crying, she said to him in a whisper: "I hope nobody can hear us."

"No one can hear you," said Claudius. "Only I hear you." And then he waited.

A few minutes later Lucillia said: "You know that I have been the Emperor's lover for some time."

He nodded. "Yes."

"And you know," she went on, "that some people in Rome consider this to be a great honor. I do not. Not any more."

He kept quiet.

"When first he noticed me, when he chose me from all the women of Rome, I too felt it to be a great honor. He feels comfortable with me. I attend to all his needs (and I use this word advisedly). But I don't love him, I never have. And now, Claudius Marcellus, I want to be free. But he hangs on. And he threatens that if I walk out on him, he will ... he will ..."

"I know," answered Claudius; "he threatens you and threatens your family."

Lucillia nodded, not even noticing that her nosebleed had stopped. Still holding the handkerchief to her nose, she continued to speak. "I have never known what true love was, or is," she whispered.

"You say you have never known?" he said.

"Yes," she almost cried through the handkerchief. "I have never known true love. I feel used. I feel that I have abused myself."

And then with open eyes she sat up and said to him: "You know that I am a Jewess, don't you."

He nodded.

"And you know what Titus did to Jerusalem?"

"Yes," he too was whispering now, "I know."

"But you cannot understand, Claudius, You cannot understand what this means to us, because you are a Roman."

He reached for her hands as if to say to her, "Yes, I do understand you, because I am a Jew too." But then he thought better of it and said nothing. All he said was: "I do understand you, Lucillia, I really do."

Lucillia went on. "I begged him. I asked him not to send the Tenth Legion to Masada. Do you understand? I did everything for him, but he still kept Silva there to do his dirty work until everything was destroyed. I had never been interested in politics," she went on. "I too am a Roman, you know. I don't know why, but in the last two or three weeks it has dawned on me that I cannot sleep with the enemy of my own people, the murderer, the butcher of my own kind. Do you understand? Do you understand, Claudius? And if you whisper a word about this to anyone, you know what will happen to me."

"I know," he answered, "nothing will happen to you."

She took the handkerchief away from her nose and gazed at him. Claudius saw that the rumors in Rome had been right: she was an exceptional beauty. She had large dark eyes, white skin, and beautiful black hair which crowned her head like a tiara.

He said: "What you are really saying to me, or rather not saying to me is that your resentment against the Emperor could not be expressed openly. So instead, your nose began to bleed. You have turned your hatred against yourself, and cannot find a way out." She nodded, weeping silently.

"But there is a way out," he said, "and you will see, we will find it together. The solution lies in you, not in me. I will help you find it, I promise you that. But your nose is no longer bleeding, and we can call them back."

Titus was very impressed with this swift cure. He said to Claudius, "I have heard about you before. From now onwards I want you to attend to my family and those near to me, you understand?"

"Yes," he bowed his head, "I understand.

VIII

He now had free entry to the Emperor's palace. Sometimes he was summoned; sometimes he went on his own initiative. He not only attended to the Emperor's family but also to the slaves, some of whom were Jews. He also went there because he wanted to see Lucillia.

When he was alone, he thought of her and her predicament. Not for a single minute did he judge her or condemn her. But he realized that he wanted her. They spent a lot of time together. Often they sat beside the pool and talked. Lucillia did most of the talking and he mainly listened; at that point this was his most important role.

One afternoon, as even the shadows were wilting in the heat of Rome, Lucillia turned to him and said: "You know, Claudius Marcellus, I could never understand why he hated the sight of blood so much. The Roman Emperor hates the sight of blood!" Hatred seemed to have appeared in her eyes as she said: "This butcher, this bastard, this murderer, hates the sight of blood! The hypocrite! So I have thought it over," she said. "If he hates it that much, I can oblige him by giving him some more. That is my only way to escape him. I know now that if I want to, I can produce a nosebleed any time. And then he will let me go. I know he will. You don't know

119

how scared he is of the slightest trace of blood, even in his food. He cannot tolerate it."

So that was the decision Lucillia made: to use the very thing, her nosebleed that had so much alarmed her that night, as a means of frightening Titus away. In the end she succeeded. The Emperor let her go. And she went into the house of the man who, in the course of time, had become her friend.

But before this happened, Abraham Claudius, mindful of the fate of the Jews, Judea and Israel, asked the Emperor what his plans were for them. Titus told him that they would all have to go, that Judea had to be destroyed as a country, that there was nothing more to discuss.

Then Abraham Claudius asked: "Before they leave, will you allow them to collect all their literature, so that they might take their books and memories along with them?"

The Emperor laughed. "Writings, words, books – they are certainly no threat to Rome."

So the few surviving Rabbis and Sages of Israel were allowed to gather the memories of what had been said and written, to set them down on paper, and to ship them off to Alexandria and to Rome and other parts of the world. And in the end the spirit of those books defeated Rome- the very books that supposedly posed no threat to Rome.

In the final reckoning, the spirit of love always prevails over the spirit of hate. Claudius Marcellus, also known by his Jewish name of Abraham, has contributed much to this ultimate triumph. His personal reward was that Lucillia became his wife, sharing his nights and his dreams, dreams of a future in which all men would be free.

In the catacombs of Rome a number of escaped slaves began to create an extraordinary, subterranean life for themselves. Even though it was forbidden to help these people in any way, Abraham Claudius Marcellus and his wife Lucillia supplied them with food, medicine, and love.

One night Abraham Claudius Marcellus was caught by the guard and beaten to death.

I wish I could have given this story a happy ending. Yet there had been happy times for the two of them, years of love, affection and growth.

So you see, had Abraham Claudius Marcellus not been beaten to death, he might not have become part of my composite Man of Auschwitz.

CHAPTER FIVE

I

After the death of her beloved husband, Avraham Claudius Marcellus, this Roman Jewish woman began to grow, both in her soul and with a new life under her heart. Lucillia was expecting a child. She felt him moving within her, and it filled her with great pleasure and great pain simultaneously. There was pleasure because there was something of the man she had come to love deeply, but also sadness because of his death and the circumstances of his dying.

During her time in the palace, the Emperor had lavished great wealth on her. She had houses (three in Rome and two villas in the country) and jewelry worth a fortune. At first she felt she ought to return all this to Titus. Then she thought about where the Emperor had gotten this vast wealth. He had gotten it from conquered nations far away, and her own people were among them. Perhaps this was a feeble attempt at self-justification in wanting to remain rich. But she felt that it was right to keep the Emperor's gifts, especially now that her husband was dead; so she would be able to choose a proper setting for her own life as well as for her son.

When her husband was still alive and she had lain in Abraham's arms during the hot summer nights of Rome, she had realized that she would never be able to love anyone as she loved him. She would never be able to give herself to another man because their love had so many aspects and colors: Her much loved Abraham had been her teacher, her brother, her friend, her father, and her soul mate.

Abraham Claudius had told her the story of Jerusalem, God's city that had, for the second time, fallen into the hands of enemies.

Whenever she visited her parents or relatives, whenever she encountered Jews who had been living in Rome for a long time, she sensed how deeply they were all affected by the loss of that distant city she had never seen, but only heard about from her husband. And everywhere the Latin slogan resounded, *'hierosolyma est perdita!'*, 'Jerusalem is destroyed!'

What could a young woman know about the meaning of all this pain?

At first she simply wished to help her fellow-Jews hundreds of miles away, and those who were slaves in Rome.

The nose bleed that had brought Abraham Claudius and her together was, as she found out after Abraham's death, very significant. She came to understand that the nosebleed had been the manifestation of her own resentment against the rape of her body by the Emperor. It had not only been her body that had been raped but also her soul. Every woman's soul is raped when she does not love her man. When a soul is raped, the body feels used and abused and will not run with the juices of springtime. It will not allow life to germinate within the secret oasis whence those juices flow. The love between her and Avraham Claudius that had started because of her nose bleed – the nose bleed that ultimately had freed her from the Roman Emperor–became more than a mere symbol to her. She began to think about the fact that frightening episodes could thus be turned into extraordinary assets.

Lucillia was still very young. She was only in her twenties and already a widow. And while a new life grew within her she asked herself, "Where do we go from here?"

While lying in her bed on that autumn evening, as she watched the leaves fall from the trees in the darkening garden and felt the tiny kicks in her womb, she remembered what her beloved husband had advised:

"If anything ever happens to me, my love, please leave this place of horror and sad memories. Please leave this place of godlessness where in the circuses, including the Circus Maximus of the Colosseum, wild animals are daily tearing apart the flesh of our people, to the amusement of the citizens of Rome, conquerors of the world. It is written in our teaching, that any man who destroys another man destroys the spirit of God Himself forever."

Remembering her husband's words, Lucillia decided to go to the place he had told her so much about. She would go to Egypt, to Alexandria, and start a new life there. She made her arrangements and left Rome for good.

II

Neither in man's unconscious, nor in space, nor indeed in history is time of any relevance. It only appears to be important to us because we are so conditioned by the limitations and structure of our existence. Naively, we believe that the time we know is the only time that exists.

Jewish history shows that this is not so. People die, yet in a sense come alive again by the transference of the soul into another person and in the continuation of life itself.

So we bid farewell to this young woman and her unborn child in Alexandria, living in a retreat overlooking a beautiful lake, where she is absorbing the ideas, ethics and beauty of Judaism, and we continue with the story of another Lucillia, hundreds of years later, in the Spanish city of *Cordoba*.

If you wish, you may regard this as the continuation of Lucillia's story and her yet unborn son. Or you might take it as a separate story. Does that matter, really?

III

Ezra ibn Bachya was born in the spring of 1050 AC in a part of Spain that belonged to the Arab Empire, whose culture, philosophy, art and science were magnificent. He was

124

born into the Golden Age of Judaism when, under Moslem rule, man was free and Jews were free to express their ideas and thoughts. They incorporated many Moslem elements into their lives and culture and, for the time being at any rate, lived peacefully in the land of the Arabs.

His mother was a Jewess who originated from Rome. About his father, who died before Ezra's birth, he knew very little. They lived the life of the rich. Lucillia was able to provide a beautiful house and a lovely garden for her young son to grow up in.

At the age of three or four, he would look up at the sky and see the clouds forming shapes and outlines, once the face of a man, then that of an animal, sometimes frightening the little boy, sometimes smiling at him. Lying in his cot for hours on end he watched the sky, the shapes of the clouds, the sun smiling at him and then vanishing as if in a game.

From time to time his mother would appear, take him out of the cot and allow him to crawl or toddle in the garden, or play with the toys made especially for him by a carpenter. Whatever he did was full of excitement and meaning. When it rained, the earth exuded a rich scent. Small as he was, he felt he must store away somewhere, somehow, this good smell. As time flew, he watched the buds ripen into fruit, and it too was exciting and good.

Beyond the excitement and the goodness of it all lay a secret that only he and of course mother knew. The mother watched every movement of her child carefully, yet she allowed him to venture forth into the world, into the world of grass and bushes and trees. He had enough freedom to explore his world. For hours he could watch the insects such as ants moving in and out, whole armies of them, carrying their food into storage for the winter months when (Mother said) the sun would not give them enough strength to survive. Ezra's world was one of unbelievable beauty; everything he experienced pleased him. Sometimes he cried in the night because the candles threw flickering shadows on the walls, images of nasty, mean men and beasts. Then mother would come and all was well again. "You know," she said, "while you sleep these bad people and angry animals turn into beautiful, beautiful fairies." And the little boy closed his eyes, thinking, "How good it is that God can turn fear into such peace!"

He was taught a language, a strange sounding language, not spoken by the other children when they met and played in the garden together. It was called Hebrew. He learned it well. By the age of fourteen he could read the Bible in the original. Not only could he read it, but he could translate almost any part from Hebrew into Spanish.

When his mother looked at her growing son, the delight in her shining eyes filled Ezra with great confidence. Now nothing was impossible for him, not even flying to the moon and to distant planets, because it was so written in his mother's smile.

By the age of seventeen Ezra could speak three languages: Arabic, Hebrew and Spanish. He had three tutors to teach him the sciences, the arts and philosophy, and he soaked it all up, wanting to learn everything about the world around him.

This was not only Judaism's Golden Age, but Ezra's too.

As an adolescent he asked his mother: "How come that there is no man around, Mother? Why haven't you provided a father for me, a man I could talk to?"

Lucillia replied: "No one could take your father's place for me. In your teachers and your friends you will find the male company that you seek. Perhaps I am selfish. Indeed you have the right to be near a man, but I too have my right to live my life as I wish."

Ezra accepted this, respecting his mother's wish to be what she wanted to be, just as he wanted to become what he wished to be.

He spoke to his mother about love, about loving a woman too. No, he had not met her as yet, but he could very well imagine her qualities.

He also spoke about what he wanted to do with his life.

"You see, Mother, from what I have learned, we Jews have been scattered around the world because our land and our holy city were destroyed. We now live in many other lands. But haven't you told me that it was my father's wish that the writings of Israel be collected, that through these writings our God-given spirit might be carried on?

Since I was a child, I have observed the trees, the sky, and the water. I have had teachers to teach me the good and precious ideas of other nations. The Arabs have a fantastic culture: just look at *Seville* and *Cordoba*, the most beautiful cities in the world! Their poets write beautiful poetry. But it is hard for me to find a book which gives an adequate and true account of my own people's history.

If you have no objections, Mother, I should like to become a recorder of our people's past. After I have died, after I am gone, others will read it, and it will live through them. The written word does not die."

Lucillia turned to her son and asked:" Beyond the reasons you have given, beyond the intellectual ability that you have always shown, do you realize why your feelings dictated these words to you? Do you know why you want to be a recorder of your people's history?"

After some silence, Ezra said: "Looking back on my life with you in this house, in this garden, I really feel contented and happy. You never prevented me from doing anything that I wanted to do. Yet I felt that your love was a control, even though it was good. You have always helped me go my way; at night you chased away the dark shadows from the wall and turned them into beautiful dreams for me.

Yet there remains a mystery. You have spoken very little about my father. Even if you did so now, Mother, the mystery would remain with me. You told me that my father had been killed in Rome. "Killed in Rome", that will not satisfy a child's imagination.

There are great historical events which shape human destiny. I want to turn the mystery into something which will

127

answer me personally; something which will be working for me, and for others, later on.

Lucillia smiled and said to her son: "Ezra, you speak as if you were a wise old man. You speak almost like the Sages of Israel."

Slowly the young man moved over to her and kissed her, saying: "But I am an old man, Mother, because I have had a wonderful youth, and because I am a Jew."

IV

On November 7th, 1923, the *Berliner Tagesblatt* wrote: "Not only have Jewish shops been plundered and Jews sought out in their homes, but some of them have had their clothes torn from their backs and been chased naked through the streets while a jeering mob ran after them and beat them."

On December 12th, 1923, *Gerhard Kaufman* was born in *Steglitz*, Berlin.

On the 23rd of April of the same year his father had died of wounds received in World War One. His wounds had become malignant and eventually both of his legs had to be amputated.

On that same day, *Hitler* announced that Germany lost the war because 'the Marxist-Democratic-Liberal-Capitalistic Jews' had stabbed the country in the back in order to aid its enemies. He claimed that the Jews were responsible for causing the war in the first place, and that Jews invented democracy in order to destroy the Germanic peoples.

Around the time that Gerhard was a boy of four, his mother expressed objections against the National Socialist Party, against its slogans, and against *Hitler* himself.

However, her brother Ludwig, a very learned man and a staunch member of the Protestant Church told Maria all about *Martin Luther*.

"For a while *Luther* tried to help the Jews against persecution by the Catholic Church, but eventually he too came to recognize the true face of Judaism."

Ludwig brought along and showed her a manifesto written by *Martin Luther* in 1544 under the title, *'Concerning the Jews and their Lies.'*

And this is what *Luther* wrote: *"Set their synagogues on fire. Whatever does not burn, should be covered or spread over with dirt, so that no man may ever see a stone or cinder of it ... Their homes should likewise be broken down and destroyed ... They shall be put under one roof, or in a stable, like gypsies, in order that they may realize that they are not masters in our land, as they boast, but miserable captives – as they complain of us before God with bitter wailing. They should be deprived of their prayer books and Talmud in which idolatry, lies, and accursed blasphemies are taught ... Their rabbis must be forbidden to teach, under the threat of death."'*

You must understand, my young German friend, that long before Hitler came onto the scene, partly because of the violent accusations and hatred of Luther against the Jews, life had become almost intolerable for many of my people.

Moses Mendelssohn (grandfather of Felix, the composer) for example, wrote in the year 1780 to a friend who was a Catholic monk as well as a philosopher:

"Everywhere in this so-called tolerant land I live so isolated through real intolerance; so beset on every side, that out of love for my own children, I lock myself up in a silk factory as in a cloister. In the evenings I take a walk with my wife and children. 'Father,' asks one of those innocent children, 'why does that fellow yell after us? Why do they throw stones at us? What have we done to them?'

'Yes, dear Father,' says another child. 'They always follow us in the street and scream at us, Jews, Jews! Father, do these people think it is a disgrace to be a Jew? And why does it matter to them?'

I close my eyes, stifle a sigh inwardly, and exclaim: 'Poor humanity! You have indeed brought things to a sorry pass.'"

It is very important, my young German friend, that you know the historical beginnings of National Socialism. So often it is said that it was the work of one man, Adolf Hitler, who brought this misery and subsequent Holocaust into the world.

Unfortunately this is not so. In 1879 for example, the population of *Bamberg, Karlsruhe, Mannheim, Heidelberg, Würzburg* and *Frankfurt-am-Main* turned against the Jews with riots, beatings and looting. Once more they raised the battle cry of the Crusaders, who in turn had inherited it from the Romans, *'Hep, hep, hep! Hierosolyma Est Perdita',* 'Jerusalem is destroyed.'

These episodes and others of their kind took place in German speaking countries and served as the prelude to *Auschwitz, Buchenwald, Maidanek* and all the other concentration camps in Nazi Germany.

It is and it will always be impossible to convey the full horror of this period. To me as a survivor, the indictment presented before the International Tribunal set up to try the Nazi War Criminals in October 1945 is valid:

"The murders and ill treatment were carried out by diverse means, including shooting, hanging, gassing, starvation, gross overcrowding, systematic under-nourishment, systematic imposition of labor tasks beyond the strength of those ordered to carry them out, inadequate provision of medical and surgical services, kicking, beatings, brutality and torture of all kinds ... Along with adults, the Nazi conspirators mercilessly destroyed even children. They killed them with their parents, in groups and alone. They killed them in children's homes and hospitals, burying them alive in graves, throwing them into flames, stabbing them with bayonets, poisoning them, conducting experiments upon them, extracting their blood for use by the German Army, throwing them into prisons and Gestapo torture chambers

and concentration camps where the children died from hunger, torture and epidemic diseases."

I, a survivor, have personally witnessed many such deaths.

V

From a town in the Federal Republic of Germany which I shall not name, because I do not want the man whom I call *Gerhard Kaufman* to be identified, there came a request for an interview. Via some intermediaries *Kaufman* sent a message that he wanted to see me.

Prior to our meeting I was told that he had been a member of the *SS* and had served, among other places, in Hungary too. The question now was whether I wanted to or could see this man, who obviously was a murderer. A killer of my own people. Perhaps of my own family.

I spent a sleepless night pondering over this request. Why, knowing who I was, where I had been, what had been done to me has this man chosen me?

In the end my curiosity won. I decided to meet him at an appointed time.

He came.

I remember the blood rushing to my head as he entered the room. When he put out his hand I did not want to take it. And yet, and yet ... I did, succumbing to the social norm of the age.

Afterwards my hand felt unclean. I kept rubbing it against my trousers as if to wipe off ... some blood perhaps.

He sat down, and I looked at him, and inwardly I prayed. I prayed that my hatred should give way to an ability to hear what this man was saying to me. I prayed for the ability to see this man as a man.

I sat there watching him. He was about my own age. Perhaps his hair was a little thinner, a little greyer than mine.

There was something in his eyes that I could not figure out. His eyes were almost glazed over, as if they belonged not to a man but to a statue or to a wax figure in *Madame Tussauds' Museum*.

He avoided my eyes. When he tried to look at me he looked if not exactly through me, then almost past me. His eyes did not seem focused at all.

What follows now is a rough reconstruction of what he told me and of what I saw simultaneously in my mind's eye.

"I am glad that you agreed to see me. I thought you wouldn't. I would have quite understood that too."

There was a long silence. I felt a vein throbbing in my right temple. He went on.

"I have a bullet in my head. It can't be removed because an operation might prove fatal. At any moment this bullet might move. If it does, I will die or be paralyzed. But it is not the bullet that I want to talk to you about."

By now I gained control over myself and over the situation.

"What is it," I asked, "that do you want to say?"

"I want to say that … that … that I cannot sleep at night. The past is haunting me. I want to say things that I cannot say, but I am here and just by being here I am saying them."

Again he sat with that glassy look in his eyes.

I said to myself: 'This man cannot speak. He utters words but he cannot speak. His soul is dead. I have never sat so near to a dead soul, to a soul that had been killed or had committed suicide. I have never been so near to death.'

I said to myself: 'I have been near physical death so many times, inside and outside the camps, but I have never been so near to a dead man.'

A shiver ran down my spine and stayed there, fixed like a stab.

"I want to say," the dead man said, "that I did not want to do those things. I want to say… " and he moved his hands

132

towards his eyes, but no tears came from those dead eyes. "I want to say that whatever you think of me, and of course you have a right to … I did try to save the life of one Hungarian Jewish woman."

A feeling akin to an electric current shot through me.

Was I sorry for him? I do not know. But it was so pathetic, so utterly pathetic, the way he said to me, 'I have saved, or I have tried to save, a Jewish woman's life.'

And out came a story of how one night he found a young Jewish girl in the street and took her home. And that was all he said.

There was a long silence.

I said: "Is that what you wanted to tell me? That you saved the life of one Jewish woman?"

He shook his head. "No. But the things that I want to say, I cannot put into words, you see."

"I see."

I saw it all right. I saw it.

November 3, 1941. *Vitebsk, Lithuania.* Some six or seven hundred men, women and children were crowded into the synagogue when the order came. A flamethrower went into action and burnt down the synagogue, and within it seven hundred people screamed and died by fire and by smoke. It is so easy to say: seven hundred people died. Seven hundred people.

But these were all individuals, with hopes, dreams, aspirations, loves and loved ones. Wearing little shoes, tiny shoes which would fit into the palm of my hand, there were little lives crying out, 'Mummy, Mummy!' And the smoke choked their tiny voices into a cry of death. And mothers threw themselves over their small children, hoping to save them by this act.

And from somewhere came the Cantor's voice, no longer singing but crying *'Hear O Israel, the Lord our God, the Lord is One!'* And then the voice choked up and then died.

The voice died.

And I saw Gerhard Kaufmann with a flamethrower standing near the synagogue, waiting for human flesh to turn into dust and ashes.

Then I saw him one summer morning. Dawn had just come, the sun rose over the horizon, and there were these graves that had been dug the night before. They had prepared these graves by torchlight, ready for those who were to be shot into them.

Columns of people were driven from somewhere. Though it was summer, it was a cold morning.

And they came in long lines, naked. Men, women and children came, all naked. Some of the men had beards, others were clean-shaven, but they all were trying to cover up their genitals with their hands, as if that were the only thing that mattered.

Mothers tried to cover up their genitals in front of their children, putting one hand over their breasts and the other over their thighs so that neither their children nor the strangers in the column of victims, nor the *SS* standing nearby should see what was meant to be private and holy, what only lovers and the beloved ought to see.

They walked along naked, and the children walked along naked, and some were carried in their mothers' arms: babies who cried and tried to suck milk.

And *Gerhard Kaufman* and several hundred other black-uniformed *SS*-men stood with a machine gun, surrounding the pit.

The officer, the *Hauptsturmführer*, smoked a cigarette and talked to his second-in-command as if everything was normal and well under the shining sun.

And the column moved slowly towards the pit.

Among those who moved towards their final hour was a young man by the name of Ezra. As he carried his young life towards its final destiny, he thought of the garden and the trees and the bushes and the flowers and his mother's beautiful face. How good it was, he thought, that she had died a natural death.

Naked, he walked ahead, trying to cover up his penis and testicles with his left hand, and pointing out some trees to a child with his right hand as if to say, 'You see, Little One, I have seen them when they were alive!'

The young man walked to the edge of the pit and stood there waiting for the bullets to come.

Gerhard Kaufman aimed his gun at Ezra's testicles. But the order to shoot did not come yet. So Ezra stood there, just stood, and waited. His lips were moving silently.

Was he praying or cursing God?

One early morning in his garden, in the shrubbery he had once explored with tiny feet, there was a girl. All night long the girl and he had lain in each other's arms. Now the sun was rising in the sky. Spent after kisses and the sweat of love, he lifted her hand to his lips.

"You are my wife."

"Yes," she answered, "I am your wife."

"You see, I have always wanted to love you on the warm earth."

"Yes," she whispered, "I have too."

And he said: "It is so good to share love with the love of my life in a place where I was once a child. All things past and present link up and usher us toward the future."

"Yes, I know."

They were alone in the house. These were the first days of their honeymoon. And the sun came up on their naked bodies, and he touched her as if to admire the miracle that was woman, and he looked at her, and she said: "I love the way you look at me."

And Ezra looked up and saw his hand covering his nakedness and saw the sun rising ever higher above the horizon and the *SS* men standing and waiting for the moment to come.

And Ezra saw that man (the man named *Gerhard Kaufman*) saw him for just one moment.

And then there was nothing any more. No memories, nothing. Not even darkness or night. Nothing. He did not even hear the click of the gun. He did not even see the others falling like felled trees. It was just one moment.

The man with the cigarette in his mouth raised his hand, then let it drop.

And that was that.

In that consulting room in the Federal Republic of Germany, when *Gerhard Kaufman* said to me that he could not speak, I saw it all.

I saw them marching away afterwards in their black uniforms. They went back and had breakfast; ham and eggs and *ersatz coffee*. They talked about the families they had left behind.

And he, *Gerhard Kaufman*, talked about his mother in Steglitz, who complained of her rheumatism and hoped that her son was well.

Sitting there, he talked about saving this Hungarian Jewish girl, and I saw the *SS* walking at night, despite orders, walking into Russian houses, bayoneting men in the abdomen and raping the women until their own souls died of suffocation.

In my mind's eye I saw how the soul had died within this man with the bullet in his head, while all around him people died whose souls will live forever. The murdered have spiritually survived their murderers.

I stood up and said to *Gerhard Kaufmann*:

"You cannot speak, yet I see it all. There is no way in which I give absolution to you, and that is what you have come for. You came to meet a Jew who has survived, so that he might tell you, by word or gesture or otherwise, that you, *Gerhard Kaufman*, have a soul. You have none."

And I walked to the window.

He stood up and moved towards the door. As he stood there, he said to me: "It was also very difficult for me, you

136

see. While there were others around, my comrades, it was not very difficult to do what we did. But when one is alone, you see, when one is alone, then some things come back to haunt you. Because, you see, deep down I knew that they were people."

Deep down he knew that they were people.

But what he was taught was that Jews were rats to be exterminated. Vermin.

A child may have smiled at him at the moment he pressed the trigger. A woman might have begged with her eyes for her child's life. Yet they were gunned into the grave. Ezra cannot ask the question: "What moral sin have I, have we committed to deserve all this?"

Well, I shall tell you what our sin as Jews was and is:

On that mountaintop God's word spoke to Abraham, and miraculously his wife conceived and bore a son.

And along with that gift we received also the truth – emanating from within and beyond the laws of the cosmos – that God is *One,* and that the universe and every pulsating or seemingly dead creature in it is alive, and that we are all children of the cosmos. We have perceived that the spirit of the Lord is ineffable, unimaginable. We have recognized that there is right and wrong on the face of this earth. We learned that there are feelings that we must cultivate just as a gardener cultivates his flowers and plants. And we know that it takes a long time for the flowers to blossom and for the fruit to ripen.

But the laws with which God put man onto this earth are the basic laws of life and of living. Beyond this earth, in the remotest recesses of the cosmos, these same laws hold true.

We have been guilty of awakening the spirit in man when man was not yet ready to receive God's spirit into his soul. So the Nazis preferred to sell their souls to the devil.

In the torture chambers of medieval Spain, in the ghettoes of France, Germany and Russia, the church foreshadowed and rehearsed what the *Third Reich* would eventually do on a vastly larger scale. No, it was not Jesus – or Yehoshua – who did it. It were those who defied his spirit and wanted to wipe it off the face of the earth. Yet we are alive. I am alive. And *Gerhard Kaufman* is lying paralyzed in his bed, because the bullet has moved in his head.

But there are others, other *Gerhard Kaufmans* who are your fathers and your brothers, your uncles and other relatives. They are still around. They keep the secrets of the burning people in that synagogue in *Vitebsk* on November 3rd, 1941, hidden deep in their minds, under the rubble of their dead souls.

Every person has a soul meant to flourish, to grow. But souls can be killed. Minds can be cured but dead souls can never be brought back to life. It is useless for you to ask the people around you, the people whose descendant you are, to tell you the story, the horrible, unspeakable story of the *Third Reich*. Like *Gerhard Kaufman*, they cannot say anything except that they did not know or did not know fully or could not have known.

Early in this letter I have told you that I don't know what I might have been capable of doing, had I been born into the German part of my family which had converted to Catholicism. I said I did not know how I would have behaved or acted in situations such as *Gerhard Kaufman's*.

No, that is not quite true. A man can endure a lot, he may have to put up with a lot, he may have to appease the conquerors a lot, may have to subdue his body a lot. But there comes a point when it is no longer a question of the survival of the body or the mind, but of the survival of the soul. At that moment, if one is condemned to spiritual death that sentence of death is eternal, to the end of time. That soul will find no resting place anywhere in the cosmos. Believe me, I know this.

Now, at that point I would have resisted and would still resist. I can prostrate my body. I can sell my mind. I might do many things I ought to be ashamed of. But what I could not do is sell my soul as *Gerhard Kaufman* sold his.

It is impossible to comprehend the enormity of six million people, of ten million people. (Six million Jews were murdered out of a total of eleven million victims of the Holocaust.) But remember those little feet of children on the edge of the pit, standing beside their mothers' naked bodies. Remember the garden in which Ezra made love, and then having to stand naked, not in the presence of love, but in the face of the ugliest hatred that mankind has ever been able to show.

These are crimes against the soul which will never be forgiven, which cannot ever be forgiven. There is no God alive in heaven or earth or beyond who can forgive the enormity that has been committed against the soul of Man.

Those who have killed have destroyed the universe of their own selves.

I spoke to you about the Man of Auschwitz with his many faces. Now you see how the elements of this composite figure have been put together. Some of the faces I have shown you; there are still some others that I will let you see. –

And, even though I hate to say this: Among the components of this composite image there are also, somewhere, the glassy eyes of *Gerhard Kaufman.*

PART FOUR

"MISSION ACCOMPLISHED"

CHAPTER SIX

I

"Great Old Man, I have asked you who you were, and you have shown me places and people. You have let me see distant places and people who were not distant at all. As I watched them enacting their lives and their deaths, I felt almost as if a part of me was within each of these people. Great Old Man, are these the components you are made of? Is that all that you are?"

Sitting under the old tree on top of the mountain, with the peaceful village slumbering in the sun down in the valley by his right hand, he answered: "I am not only that which I have shown you. I am you too, you know: your past, your present, and in a sense also your future. That is why I can tell you things that have meaning for you. That is why you were wrong in thinking that I was talking *at* you, lecturing you. How could I do that, seeing that the thoughts I am uttering are particles of your own life too? I am you but, as you have noticed, more than you. There are many more components from the span of space and time that add up to me, this old man you see sitting under a tree on a mountain top."

I sat there on the sun-warmed earth looking at him, and I said:

"The people you have shown me all have had meaningful lives. They all suffered pain and all found some truth. But did all of them have to come to a tragic end? Ultimately, must there be pain, and then arising from pain recognition of life and love and beauty, and then an end in tragedy? Isn't there a part of you which does not end in death, in torture, in humiliation?"

He thought for some time. His eyes gazed beyond the horizon, and then returned to mine.

"Those who are chosen, you know, are not only chosen for life but for what you call death too. Life and death are but two sides of the same coin. You want to live a life of contentment, which is only natural. Yet do you really think that one can have contentment without paying the price? Can there be day without night? Can there be spring without autumn and winter? And conversely too, can there be winter without a spring to follow it, again and again?"

I pondered this for a very long time without saying a word. My thoughts and feelings were racing very fast. I saw birds taking off in the autumn, before winter's advent, birds in their hundreds and thousands flying south from the shores of Europe to find a warmer climate while our winter rages.

Once in Regent's Park I saw them rise and wheel around in great circles over the trees, then suddenly change their direction to the south, and fly off. A friend standing next to me said: "They will come back in spring."

I saw them, countless little fluttering wings, following their leader. And I thought, "Yes, they will be back in spring. But how many will die on the way there or on the way back?"

And on a lovely spring day I was standing there as they returned. This time they flew, not in a single vast cloud, but in smaller flocks, now one, then another, then yet another. And I felt a renewal of spring in my heart too.

"Here you are, my little birds that flew away, who came back and brought back the hope of summer. But how many have you lost on your journey? What price have *they* paid so that *you* who survived may come back?"

The birds did not reply. But my heart answered on the birds' behalf:

"I feel the spring within me, because your return makes me anticipate lazy, sunny days to come. Your song will awaken me in the morning and rock me to sleep at night. They are the same songs as in the days of the past, last year's spring, and the year before, and hundreds and thousands of

141

years before. You come and go according to the laws of your nature and instincts. But you always return. And yet you too had to pay the price."

I turned to the Great Old Man and said:

"I had a vision just now, of what you really mean by life and death. In reality you are speaking of two distinct things. You speak of the individual who lives and dies. And then you speak of the community, of the House of Israel which after every persecution, even after this last Holocaust, makes a comeback and brings forth a new, warm spring. But is it worthwhile for so many individuals to suffer pain and agony so that the rest may return? Those naked men and women at the edge of the pit, did they care that one day I and a few others will come back from the jaws of death? If I were standing before a firing squad, what kind of consolation would it be for me to say, 'Yes, but others will live on?' Isn't my life the only one that exists for me?"

There were tears trembling in his eyes as he looked deep into mine.

"Tell me this as honestly as you can: If you were to face a violent death at the hand of any enemy today, would it not matter to you to know that the idea, the ideal you have lived for and must now die for, will live on after your death? Would you rather that the idea itself died along with you? Beyond the preservation of your own individual life (concerning which you had no choice), would you not choose a living idea over a dead one?"

And I said to him: "If I had my son and my daughter standing naked at my side facing death, do you really think that I would concern myself with such thoughts and feelings?"

After a pause, he said: "No, your thoughts and feelings at that point may very well be a concern, an agony over yourself and your children. That is understandable. But if, beyond the fear of facing impending death, you had time to think about that which never dies, if you knew that there were certain ideas that would never die and that you were intermeshed

142

with those ideas through all eternity, wouldn't you rather choose to live on through those ideals than die along with them?"

"Great Old Man, I am a survivor. To me life is very precious, and the ideal of the House of Israel is also very precious. But you are talking about two different truths. One is my own individual life. The other is the collectivity of life itself, just as with the birds in Regent's Park a few moments ago, leaving in the autumn, only to return in spring. Tonight, when the birds sing, they may not be the same birds as last year."

The Old Man asked: "Did you ever think of that before this very moment?"

"What?"

"That the birds that sing outside your window are not the same birds?"

"No," I said, "I have never thought of it before this moment."

"And now that you have thought of it," he went on, "search your heart and tell me truthfully: does it matter to you whether they are the same birds that sing?"

"No," I answered, "the truth is that it doesn't matter."

The Old Man continued: "You may weep with one eye for the birds that were lost along the way. But shouldn't you smile and laugh with the other, seeing that the birds that did come back still sing the same song of the centuries?"

"Yes."

Again silence lay between us. I sensed the gentle breeze caressing my skin and stirring my hair and breathing warmly at my eyes. I began to understand a mystery that hitherto I could not comprehend. Lives may come and go, but instincts implanted deep in creatures and ideas implanted deep in men live on. And someone, somehow, will take care of all those who fall for the sake of others – others who may arrive.

I asked: "Does He care about the fallen ones? What is on the other side of the coin, the side we call death?"

A warm gust of southerly wind came up. Down below, in the village slumbering in the sun, the smoke rising from the chimneys wafted with the wind.

"You want me to tell you about death. You want me to tell you about the other side of the coin, the side you are not meant to see?"

"Yes," I said, "tell me about it."

"Even if you are not meant to see it?"

"What kind of joke is it to tell a survivor who lost six million of his kindred that I am not supposed to see the other side of death? I have faced that side a thousand times."

"Are you challenging the will of God?"

"Yes, I challenge the will of God."

"All right," he said quietly. "I'll tell you."

II

"It all has to do with love."

III

London, November 4th, 1955. At eleven o'clock there was a knock on my door. I was sitting in my consulting room attending to some letters. At that time I was working with people who had lost their purpose in living and who had no job, no work to do.

I said: "Come in."

At first a dog appeared, and then a young woman followed. She was blind and wore dark glasses.

Carefully and gently the dog led her to a chair. I quickly got up and helped her sit down. She looked like in her late twenties, and with her lovely face and her long brown hair she looked quite attractive.

She sat in her chair for some time and the dog lay down at her feet.

I did not interrupt her silence.

"I want to talk to you," she said at last.

144

"Yes?"

"I need to talk to someone."

"Yes," I said again.

"I lost my sight about four months ago. I have diabetes; I've had it since I was a child. And then it began to happen. At first it was a blur. What I could see became like some abstract paintings on a moving wall. Then one night I saw the light go out for the last time."

There was silence between us. Then she went on:

"I was brought up on a farm in the country. When I was young, well, when I was a child, I found out that something was very, very wrong. My parents' anxiety seeped into me, and like a piece of blotting paper, I soaked up their fears. I lived with fear without knowing what it was all about. Of course they knew that I was a diabetic, and they also knew what the consequences of that illness were and would be in the future.

I want to tell you something that I have never told anyone. When I was twelve or thirteen, I was deeply in love with a young man and I gave myself to him. An old-fashioned expression, I know, yet that was how it was. I gave myself to him. When we were together, very close, flesh to flesh, for the first time that unknown fear left me. I thought that was the secret. Whenever I went to be with him, the fear and the unspeakable tensions went away. I clung to him like someone drowning clings to life."

The dog stirred; someone was passing by outside in the corridor.

She put on her hat, then took it off again and put it down on the floor.

I did not know what to say. It was a strange encounter. This lovely young woman had walked in, sat down, and started to tell me something so important that she had never told anyone else in her life before. I did not quite understand what I was supposed to do. Ought I perhaps to say something wise, or ask some questions? A tiny flicker of a voice within me said: 'Be quiet. Wait. This is her time, not yours. This is her story, her life, not yours. You must be patient.'

At the same time I was acutely aware that this blind woman could sense my mood more accurately than sighted people could. From my voice, my nervous cough, my fidgeting in my chair, she could tell what was going on within me.

She said: "You are wondering why I came."

I said: "You wanted to talk to someone. You have said so."

She said: "Yes, but why to you? What do you think?"

I said: "I don't know why it should be me."

"Don't you really?" she added.

I said: "No, I am sorry. I am glad that you came. But I don't know why it was me you came to."

Then she said: "Because you, Mr. Heimler, you have died. And by the grace of God you have been resurrected and here you are. I cannot talk to the living because they would not understand what I am going to say. I read in the papers about you and about your past experiences. So I came to you."

A year earlier, when I had been appointed to my position, the local paper printed an article about my experiences in the camps, about my conclusions, about the way I was at that time viewing my past and present and about my plans for the future. I told the interviewer that I was seeking ways to use these experiences in order to help people rather than to hurt them. It was this part that got through to her. Her mother used to read the paper to her every day, and she read her that article. It was the time when she could still see those vague shades moving around her, when her mind was clouded by the fear of losing the sights of this world.

She continued her story. When she realized that she was losing her sight, although at that point she could still discern some shadowy figures with her eyes, she would move around the house touching every object – furniture, cups, glasses – so

146

as to prepare herself for the long night that would follow her brief days in the sun. By now she had also been told the truth about her life expectancy. She did not have that much life left to live. Usually people who became diabetic in childhood did not live much more than some ten or fifteen years after the onset of blindness. Fully knowing that the end was in sight, what should she do with those precious few years still remaining?

"You are concerned with people who are unemployed. Well, I am. What do you think I can do?"

The question came sharply and directly. Immediately I tried to think of some kind of answer. Again the small voice within me said: 'Be quiet. Wait. This is her time. This is her life.'

There was a silence between us. But within me a feeling began to flare up, as on a winter night when a new log is put on top of the embers. The glow became a flame. Something came alight within me, a feeling I had known before but have not felt so strongly for quite some time. It was not pity that filled my soul, though at first I mistook it for that. It was something else. ... It was the bright, white light of love, a light that wanted to give, because the light is there to give.

During my time in the concentration camp I myself went through a few days of what I now describe as hysterical blindness. My world collapsed into utter darkness, and then a Rabbi stood beside me and held my hand. It was this pulsating, warm hand that allayed my panic; his love and care eventually restored my sight. I have described this event in my book *Night of the Mist*. This episode and many others came to my mind.

Here I was, seeing her, yet she could not see me. After the world had almost been burnt to cinders, here I was, able to see shapes and colors, the typewriter and the door and the paintings on the walls and the chairs and the carpet and the dog. And all that was no longer hers to see. But the light within me was not kindled by the fact that I could see while

147

she could not, that I experienced something and she did not. That was not it at all.

Rather, my life had a purpose now, having survived had a purpose now, and that purpose was to give.

And a tiny little voice inside me said:

'Giving in silence is best. But you must let her know that you care.'

Words? At times words are useless. Shall I say to her, 'We are going to sort this out together.'? Or 'I care.' Shall I say, 'I experience a light within me which is aflame like fire and wants nothing but to give?' Perhaps. But not yet; it is too early.

Week after week she came, brought by her parents and sometimes by her brother. With the help of her dog she walked up the two flights of stairs.

Then she spoke. She had a lot to say.

Enclosed for many years within the walls of her home, within the walls of a loving family, she wanted to reach out towards the world. She felt she had something to offer. "Now that my blindness is total," she said, "I have something to give."

That stunned me. It shouldn't have, but it did. This woman who could not see wanted to give and had something to give, and precisely because she could not see, she was now able to give.

I asked: "You want to give. What do you want to give? And to whom?"

Her voice was firm yet very feminine as she said:

"I want to give my fear and the knowledge I gained through that. I want to give my experiences of having been enclosed within the walls of my house. But more than that: I want to give something from within me, which might help others who must face the final darkness. If you can help me find a way to do so, not only will I be grateful to you, but I will have fulfilled my destiny. How shall I put it? I may have been put into the world to do just this. *My blindness is the present which I can give to those who are going blind."*

148

And so we began. She spoke and I listened. At the end of each hour I tried to interpret for her the meaning of what she had been saying. But soon it became clear that almost always she was saying the same thing. All I had to do was to listen to her words and to the meaning she seemed to give to them: 'Help me get the training which will enable me to do the same kind of work you are doing. I will not let you down. I will not let anyone down.'

And so began the story of her helping the blind. She enrolled and got the training she needed. I cannot say anything more without revealing her identity. For many years, until the end of her life, she devoted her time to supporting the blind.

As we got to know each other better, I could share some of my own experiences of life with her. It was not so much a matter of my telling anecdotes to her so as to fill the gap of empty moments. Rather, I felt it appropriate for one human being to share with another their common experiences of fear and love.

Eventually we returned to where we had started, to the deep secret of her life, to how in those early years when she could still see, she once opened herself to a young man's love. She felt that as long as this love was still within her, it would keep her not only alive but healthy as well. Love, she thought, would ward off all disease. That particular youthful adoration had faded away. But love itself remained and flourished within her.

Just as everything became dark, without shapes or contours, she began to see – to truly see – for the first time.

IV

I told the Old Man of this story which began in 1955 and led up to the stage where she could use her handicap as an asset in life. I asked him:

"Is this what you mean by 'the other side of the coin'? Do you mean to say that loving and the ability to give must include perhaps dying too, as an act of love? Am I too simple or too stupid in supposing that perhaps the dying can help the living in some way? And if, as I have experienced then and ever since, love is behind it all, are you saying that this flame can never be put out in those whose soul remains alive? Is that what we humans are not supposed to see?"

He answered: "It is not a matter of what we are supposed to see. It is a question of not being able to see. It is a form of blindness."

"So, Great Man, what you are saying is that love consists of giving, that giving is the essence of loving itself. You intimate that those among us who cannot love cannot experience life itself. You are telling me that all those ancestors of mine and all the components who make up your being have offered the ultimate sacrifice (though not necessarily by choice) by giving up their lives for the sake of love, the love of an idea or an ideal. And this love, you say, is perennial like the flight of birds. Though individual birds may drop into the sea and die, the idea of the survival of their journey will live on for ever and ever, as long as birds exist.

So are you saying that this ultimate gesture of giving up life itself expresses and perpetuates the highest form of love?"

And he answered: "You know that this is so."

The wind mussed my hair playfully as I again turned to him and asked:

"Why is it the will of God that we should not see the other side of the coin, the side which is death?"

And he answered: "You must find what you refer to as the flame, not in death where it is unattainable, but in life. The will of God is that you find this glow of love here and now."

V

In July 1945, in my hometown of Szombathely – named Savaria by the Romans -, in Western Hungary, a man lay sleepless on his bed. It was his first night back at home, having just returned from the death camps. He was allocated a flat by the authorities, and he occupied one room in it. People unknown to him lived in the other rooms.

It was a hot night. The stars shone brightly. From his bed he could see a sequent of the sky, and he was reminded of his youth and childhood. Yet unlike then, now there was a strange solitude and loneliness around him and within him. He felt as though he were suspended midair in that dark space out there, as though he were imprisoned in an invisible glass cage from which he couldn't break out. On that strange night, the first night after his return, he felt that there was no one to whom he could talk.

Then there was a knock on his door. It was around one o'clock or so. He turned the key and opened the door and there, on the threshold, stood a young woman of about his own age.

"My name is Ruth," she said. "I live in the room next to yours. The walls are so thin that I could hear you tossing and turning in your bed. It is an old bed," she said smiling, "you can hear every movement."

"Come in," the young man said, and she did.

As he moved towards the switch, Ruth said: "Don't put on the light. The light from outside is enough. Anyway, I have brought a candle with me. I always keep a candle in this place because sometimes there are power cuts."

She lit the candle and sat down on the edge of the bed. Apart from a chair and a very small table, there was no other furniture in the room. They looked at each other in the twilight of the candle flame.

'She is an attractive girl', he thought. As she looked at him, she found him much older than his age of twenty four years.

"I too was there," she said.

"Were you?"

"Yes, I was there for almost a year."

"And where was 'there'? he asked.

Ruth said: "The same places. The same time."

"Auschwitz, Buchenwald?" he asked.

"Not Buchenwald, but Auschwitz, yes. Later on it was … Do you mind that I came in here?"

"No," he answered, "I am glad. I feel very much alone."

"Yes," she said after some thought, "I too. But not for long now."

"What does that mean?" he asked.

"I am on my way to Palestine. There I won't be alone any more."

He lay down on his bed again, while she was still sitting on its edge. The candle light flickered from the table. For a long while no words were spoken. A shooting star blazed across the sky and then there was darkness, yet the sparkling stars shimmered for a long, long time.

"Strange," he thought to himself, not uttering a word, "strange how alone I still feel."

And she thought: "I feel cold. I would like to lie beside him so that we could keep each other warm." But she did not dare to ask. So there they were, he alone with his loneliness, and she shivering in the hot night.

"Do you want me to go?" she asked eventually.

"No, stay!"

A car passed by. They both listened to the roar of the engine until it died down in the distance. She said: "Don't you mind, really, that I am here?"

"No." he said. "I don't mind."

He wanted to say something polite like 'I am glad you are here', or 'It is better like this, we are not alone', but he could not say it. He was not yet used to intimate company. He felt alone, and so did she.

Ruth said: "I haven't had a period for about a year. I don't feel like a woman any more."

Now something stirred in him. Something moved upwards from the pit of his stomach, then stopped. Politely he asked: "Why is that?"

"Why is what?"

"That you haven't had a period for a year."

Ruth said: "None of us had. Women did not have periods in the camps, you know."

He did not know. And again, politely, he asked: "And why is that?"

She became a little irritable. "Why, why, why," she responded. "We didn't. Don't ask me for deep psychological explanations. I don't know." She thought: 'That was real, the feeling was real.' Her irritability was real. For about a year she had buried her irritability and all her other feelings too. And now, here by the light of a candle in a room temporarily allocated for the benefit of transients, she was growing impatient with this stranger, this young man who looked so much older than his age.

He sat up and, like some kind of robot or machine, he reached out and put his arm around her shoulders:

"I am sorry, I did not mean to …"

"I know," she said quietly, sadly. "You didn't. Why should you? In a way you are my brother."

Now it started again, this feeling from the pit of his stomach. It resembled a spark or an electric current that rose directly to his head and lodged between his eyes. It was not a bad feeling, though it felt strange. It was a sensation he had not known before. Something had started …. As if some huge, intricate electric machine was starting up.

He said: "I don't feel like a man, either."

This young woman had never heard such a confession from a man before. She wanted to ask why, but then she remembered how impatient she had been with him; so she kept quiet.

Instead she put her hand on his knees, and there they continued to sit on the edge of the bed by the flickering candle light in the night.

153

"I want to lie down," said Ruth.

"All right," said the young man, "lie down."

And the two of them lay down on that strange old bed which creaked at every movement. There they lay, side by side, separated by the night which spread both within them and outside of them.

They did not know how much time had passed until a distant church bell tolled three times. It was three o'clock in the morning.

Even though they had been together for quite some time, they still felt very much alone.

She thought: "I must ask him about what he had said about not being a man, about not feeling like a man - but how?"

When she had gathered up enough courage she asked: "You say that you don't feel like a man. How is that?"

"They gave us some injections, and the rumor was that they made us, well, impotent."

"Yes," Ruth said, "they performed some experiments with us too. Thank God, not with me. But I haven't had a period for a year, and I really don't know what is going to happen, whether I will ever have one again."

He wanted to reply: "Yes, you will!" but he knew that this would ring false; it would not come from his heart. So he kept quiet.

Ruth reached for both his hands, which were very cold.

So they lay there until the church bell struck the half-hour. Half past three. Somewhere on the far horizon a touch of pink began to spread, just a touch. She got up and, as if this were the most important and urgent thing to do, she put out the candle. Then she came back and lay down again. By now the air had cooled down somewhat, so she took off her shoes and crept under the blanket. He stayed outside the blanket and nothing stirred inside him.

She turned to him and said: "I want to sleep, do you?"

"I don't know." And then he stayed silent and motionless and watched the colors of morning that spread across the sky. She slept; but he did not.

In the growing daylight he looked at her face.

Her face bore the marks of starvation, just as his own did. Her bones were jutting through the skin. 'Poor girl, he thought, poor girl, what have you done to deserve all this?'

He went on watching her carefully. And then, half sitting, half lying, he too fell asleep on that bed.

When she opened her eyes and saw him sleeping, she carefully sat up, so as not to wake him, and spread the blanket over him. This time it was she who was watching his face. 'Not to feel like a man, ... not to feel like a woman,' she thought. 'What have they done to us?'

A feeling as warm as a hot spring leaping from the earth began to spread within her. She was moved to touch his head and his face with great gentleness. As she did so, she felt vibrations within herself that she had not sensed for a long, long time...

Then he woke up, apparently conscious of the last few moments, and said:

"Come back." And she did.

Once more her hands were touching his head. Not much hair had grown back as yet on his head that had been shaven (as were all men) in the camps. Gently she caressed him. He did not stir. He did not feel anything at all. He just lay there and fell asleep again.

She gazed at the head of this strange boy whom she had never seen before and felt something in her belly that was neither erotic nor sexual but rather as if something had moved. Yes, something moved. Like when a woman first feels the tiny kicks of her unborn child within her body. Yet how could it be that? The warmth of this feeling was of a different kind. It was ... love.

The feeling was deep, so deep that for some moments she could do nothing but weep. And in order not to wake him, she

155

silently let her tears roll down her face. Yet he woke up when they touched him, and he kissed her tears away.

And as he did so, the salty tears brought back a memory to him. 'What was it?' he wondered. 'It must have taken place a very, very long time ago. Did Mother cry, or was it the nurse? Who did?'

Now he felt hunger contracting his stomach, and he wanted to ask Ruth if she had something to eat in her room, as he did not have anything in his place.

But before he could say something - as if she was reading his mind-, she sat up and asked: "Are you hungry?"

He nodded and smiled, and she smiled through her tears.

"Come!" she said, and they walked over into the other room. It too looked bare and desolate. But now they were not alone anymore; now there were the two of them.

She made coffee and offered him bread and butter and jam. And he ate. He ate with an appetite he had not known for a very long time.

When sated, he asked: "Do you have anything to do today?"

She laughed. "What could there be to do? My transport doesn't leave for another few days. I am *free*." And as if she suddenly understood the meaning of what she had just said, she repeated: "Yes, I am free, free, FREE!"

He smiled at her and said: "Come, let's go back to bed."

"Here," said Ruth.

"All right, here."

Now he began to speak.

"You wanted to know," he said, "what I am afraid of. Well, I am afraid that I can never ... make love again."

She wanted to say: "Oh, you silly thing," but she kept quiet.

"You see, if a man feels that, he feels that he is nothing. You might as well blow out your brains. That is what it feels like."

"I think", she said, "it has to do with something else. I think it isn't a question of, how shall I put it ... your body at all. It is not a question of your body. It is your … your mind, or … I don't know. It is not your body."

She looked at him and said again: "No, no. It is not your body, you know."

And as she looked at him with admiration and said: 'It is not your body, you know', that feeling, that spark, that electricity moved again. But this time it did not go upwards, towards his head.

Did pity start it all? Or was it the appreciation he read in her eyes which said to him, 'You are okay; don't be afraid'?

He asked: "May I kiss you?"

And Ruth opened her mouth and said: "I'll bite you."

Now that brought back a lot of memories, of teasing and games and girls.

"If you do, he said, "I'll bite you back."

"We'll see," she said. And they both laughed, laughed together for the first time.

The sun was shining high in the sky. It was a beautiful summer day, and … they were happy.

The chimes of the church rang ten. And there they lay, facing each other.

"You have been crying?" he asked.

"You silly thing," she said to him, "I was crying because I felt that … well, I felt that I was a woman again."

"How?

"Well," she answered, "because of *you*."

Did it happen like this, when Adam first set eyes on Eve? Did she say, 'Because of *you* the world was created. A new world, with new dimensions, full of new colors'?

When Ruth said 'Because of *you*', there was a moment of stillness within his body, and then he felt that he was a man. And she felt it too.

They lay there motionless for a while as if the moment were so precious that they had to keep it forever and ever.

157

Now his turn came to allow his tears to run free. In front of a woman? Yes, yes. Where else? Now, while she was gently holding him, she kissed away *his* tears. "

VI

I visited Israel for the second time in the summer of 1971. During my first visit there I was overwhelmed by an atmosphere of delight, a feeling of belonging to the earth and to the sky, to the citrus trees and to the smell of the fruit, but first and foremost to the places where my ancestors had worked, cried and prayed.

When I had first visited the Land of Israel, I had taken my son with me, so that he might witness my feelings and thoughts, hoping that these impressions would be forever implanted in his young mind.

At the time of my second visit, he had already spent about a year in Jerusalem, studying at the Hebrew University.

This time, my second wife, Lily, came along too. On my previous trip, the *kotel,* the Western Wall of the Temple in Jerusalem, was not yet in Jewish hands. It was still under Jordanian rule. No Jew was allowed to pass through the *Mandelbaum Gate,* to enter the Old City and visit the remains of this historic place, our holiest remnant from ancestral times.

We arrived tired on a warm day in June 1971. Although it was late at night, my first journey was to the *kotel,* the Western Wall. It was long past midnight, yet there were still many people around, people who had come to pray for health, for happiness and for other blessings to the unseen God of Israel. Spotlights bathed the Wall in almost daylight brilliance. Above the Wall, on the surrounding elevations, just barely visible, Israeli soldiers stood guard with machine guns. They were not there to kill or to threaten or to intimidate, but simply to keep watch over Israel's most precious holy place, the Wall that symbolized the Temple of

Jerusalem which had been devastated first by he Babylonians and then by the Romans. So now this survivor stood facing the symbol, the symbol both of the land and the spirit of Israel.

As I moved nearer to the Wall, I started to tremble. I have never experienced this kind of tremor before. It started somewhere deep within me; even my lips were twitching, and I felt my teeth chattering, as the trembling possessed me. My whole body was shaking. My knees were weak as I walked over to the Wall. The stones were warm to my touch.

Tears flooded my eyes, and I prayed:

"God of Israel and of the Universe. I thank You for granting me this moment for which my people, and I among them, have been waiting for almost two thousand years. I thank You for my life, for bringing me out of the hell of hells. I thank You for my life that I can use to help others. I thank You for giving me my family. I thank You for allowing me to work for mankind. I thank You, my God."

I stood there and cried. I cried into the night the words which had been on my ancestors' lips when they died all over the world: in the gas chambers, at the mass graves of Russia and Poland, and further back in the centuries in the torture chambers of the Holy Inquisition at the hand of priests of the Church of Rome, at massacres initiated by *Martin Luther* and his followers, and during pogroms ordered by Tsars. I cried aloud:

"Hear O Israel, the Lord our God, the Lord is One. Blessed be his Name forever and ever."

Then, standing there, I silently recited *Kaddish,* the prayer for the dead. I stood beside the Wall and leaned my head against it. I felt the throbbing in my head and the warmth radiating from the Wall.

A legend holds that however hot it is in the Land of Israel, the Wall is always damp, as though the Wall itself were weeping. As I moved away my head, I felt the dampness. I touched the Wall as a lover who touches the body of his beloved in a moment - not of ecstasy, but of peace. And I

159

kissed the Wall with the kiss of a lover whose lost beloved has returned.

An ageless tradition teaches that if you make a secret wish when you visit the *kotel* for the first time, God will grant it. I made my secret wish.

The spotlights were still shining bright as I turned around and saw the soldiers standing above, like children taking care of their parents.

These were my people. After all that misery, after all those years I had come home to my land. Here I was, a symbol of the resurrection of the people of Israel.

I don't know how long I stood there.

When I had finished my prayers and meditations, I slowly stepped backwards, still facing the Wall, as if in the presence of a king. Indeed, the King of Kings.

This part of Jerusalem is the symbol of everything that we have lived for and died for. It is a symbol of death, but also of resurrection. A miracle has taken place here. We have returned from exile from the four corners of the world – as God has promised –, and this time we shall stay. We shall stay however great the dangers are. We shall stay and fulfill the prophesy that had been given to our forefathers Abraham, Isaac and Jacob.

I have always felt deep inside me that I was a Jew. But not until that moment when I stood there in the warm night under the spotlights and touched the stones of the *kotel* did I realize just how deeply I felt about my Jewish heritage.

Israel is a land of miracles. What greater miracle can there be than for a nation that had lost its land, to return to its original place and re-establish its independence? No words of prose or poetry can adequately express this feeling of total identity with two thousand years of persecution, beauty, defeat and ultimate victory. Only prayers.

A prayer came to mind; you might call it a poem if you wish. I wrote it in 1942, in the middle of the war. And as I walked away from the *kotel*, its words reverberated in my heart:

160

"How good it is that one can pray so simply
No need to go afar to icy shrines
Remote from heart, too jostling close to men.
I pray ... that is: my thoughts to God
I seek to link, and say, "Forgive!"
And "Thank You" too.
I saw you white in childhood. Long-bearded
As depicted on a mural in some
Baker's shop. I thank You for Your image
Which I shall cherish and fondly rediscover
In every God-exploring prayer.
Sometimes awake
I saw You within wide-eyed wonder-lakes
Where mossy weeds swayed greenly in the deep
Their colors calling meadows to my mind.
I saw You ... I saw You ... Therefore I thank
You for all.
I pray – and send into the endless waves
My feeble word
To Man ... to Heart ... to Wonder."

(Translated from the original Hungarian by
Rabbi Dr. André Ungar)

VII

I now continue the story of Ruth and her newly found companion, and of the love they discovered one night in the summer of 1945 in my home town of Szombathely.

Here were two people, a man and a woman, whose identity had been shaken to the core. By some miracle, they found each other and some unity for one night.

I had not known Ruth before she had come to our town on her way to Palestine. I had not known her until the morning when I knocked at his door and found her sitting on the bed with my friend whose name was Alexander Benedict.

At that point they did not tell me their story. But after Ruth was gone, Alex told it to me many, many times.

As it happened, quite unexpectedly, the message for Ruth to leave for Palestine arrived that very afternoon. I was there in the flat when the messenger arrived from the Jewish organization that was arranging for the *aliya*, the emigration to Palestine, which was at that point still illegal.

When the messenger came, Ruth packed her meager belongings, stood in front of Alex and kissed his face as if he were her brother, father or son. He embraced her in similar fashion and then she left without even looking back.

There we were in the empty flat, Alex and I.

An hour later Alex suddenly sat up on the bed and said in alarm:

"Jancsi, I only know her first name, I don't know who she is ... and she doesn't know my name either." We got up. Quickly he got dressed and hurried to the synagogue from where the group was to have left. But they had gone already.

And there were Alex and I in the deepening shadows of the summer afternoon, and he said: "I let her go."

I said: "Yes, you did."

"I will never see her again."

I kept quiet. After some thought, I said:

"You could, you know, if you followed her in the next group."

"No," he said, "I won't find her. Besides, I have some other plans, I always had. I want to go to the West. Israel ... Israel needs healthy people, men who can fight for her survival. Jancsi, I've had enough."

I have known Alex since we were children. We had played together a lot. We quarreled and fought and argued a lot. We chased after girls a lot. It wasn't and it isn't my custom to probe into people's private lives unless they volunteer for it; so I did not ask him what this young woman meant to him. Quite obviously, she meant a great deal.

162

He said: "And now I have to go back to the flat, and I will be alone there, and then one day I will begin to pack my things and go off in the opposite direction ... Oh God, what is this life all about?"

"I could stay with you for the night," I responded, not quite understanding what he meant.

But he said: "No, no, Jancsi. I think I need to be alone. That woman", then he changed the word, "That girl has given me something for the future. She has given me a precious gift, and I will never be able to return it."

"What gift?"

"I'll tell you one day; but not now."

Then we went our separate ways. He went back to his empty room, and I to mine.

I met Ruth only this once, and then for only a short time on that pivotal afternoon when she left.

I saw a lot more of my friend before he finally arranged his visa and other papers to go to the United States. By autumn he too was gone. I did not hear from him for a long time, ... but we did meet again. I shall tell you later how that came about.

Such things were happening all the time then. People were coming and going and then they were gone. Many people wanted to leave the land that had betrayed them and had surrendered them into the hands of the enemy.

Israel is the Land of Miracles.

One morning during our visit to Jerusalem, my wife Lily and my son George climbed up the Mount of Olives (Do you remember it? Yehoshua had taught there: Jesus, that is). It was a hot day. I don't enjoy climbing hills or mountains in the heat because of my back injury.

Therefore I decided to sit in a café instead, in the cool morning air of Jerusalem, and try to read a Hebrew newspaper. Reading Hebrew was a strange experience for me: I had only studied Biblical Hebrew, not the modern version. So I had to conjecture how the ancient word for 'thunder' gave rise to the modern term for 'telegram'. It was fun to try to figure things out in that fashion.

In the course of the days preceding my arrival some papers had printed articles about me and my work, including some photographs. They described my work and my aims, and how all this might be applied in the State of Israel. They mentioned that I was to lecture at the Hebrew University for a few days. As yet I had not begun to do so; I had a few days of glorious doing nothing in God's Holy City.

So there I sat in the café reading the paper when suddenly I noticed a young man of just about my son's age, a soldier, an officer in the Israeli Army, accompanied by a middle-aged woman. They sat down. The woman said something in Hebrew to her son, who went off to find the waiter. Suddenly she called after him in Hungarian: "But tell him, without milk, please!"

I looked up at her face. ... It was Ruth.

Usually I don't remember names. Names are totally irrelevant to me, but I don't easily forget a face. Seeing Ruth with this young soldier of my own son's age, I wanted to be sure. But actually I had no doubts, no doubts at all.

Twenty six years had passed since that fateful –at least for Alex fateful – afternoon in Szombathely. Still weeping over the loss of Ruth, he had left the town, God only knows where he was going,… to discover the New World, to find himself.

And here was Ruth with …

I walked over and asked gently: "Ruth?"

The middle-aged woman's face had still retained its contours although it had filled out somewhat. She looked at me and said "*Ken*?" ('Yes', in Hebrew).

I continued in Hungarian: "Ruth, you will not remember me, you will not even remember my name. But do you remember that afternoon in Szombathely in the summer of 1945?" And remembering that Alex told me she did not know

164

his name either, I added: "The flat you left from to go on *aliyah*?"

I had meant no harm, but suddenly I feared that she might faint. Her face went white, her lips began to tremble, and I wondered what in heaven's name I had done. The young man came back; he was (now I saw) older than my son.

"What is it, Mother?" he said in Hebrew. He glared at me as if he was about to throw himself at me. God only knows that I was in no mood to be attacked by this young tiger.

"Who are you?" he asked in Hebrew.

I answered in Hungarian: "I am someone who has known your mother a long time ago."

Now Ruth had regained her senses and said to her son: "It's all right. It is all right. This man is a friend ... Listen, listen ... Ezra, please! Would you mind leaving us alone? I want to speak to him in private."

Ezra glanced at the coffee cups the waiter had just put before them and said: "But..."; and he pointed at the cup, as if to say, 'But I haven't drunk my coffee yet!'

With a faint smile his mother said, "I'll get you another one later. You must go back anyway. I'll tell you all about it."

The young officer gave me an unfriendly look and said reluctantly: "Okay, if you say so." Then he saluted me, none too cordially, and left.

My eyes followed him. A fine, nice boy, blond and blue eyed, like a specimen out of an Aryan picture book.

Ruth invited me to sit down.

"I didn't mean to frighten you, you know."

"Yes, I know."

Then she reached out and touched my hand as she said: "I just barely remember you. I only remember that someone came that afternoon. - So it was you..."

"Yes, it was me."

A paper was lying in front of her. I saw my photograph staring up from the open page. In order to explain, a little apologetically, what I was doing in Jerusalem, I pointed at the accompanying article. She hardly glanced at it and said:

165

"Ah, so you have become famous!"

She said it without interest, however. Her curiosity was elsewhere. It was abundantly clear that if I had any significance to her at all it was not for my own sake.

Almost mechanically she put her son's coffee in front of me and, without any preliminaries, she asked: "How is he? Where is he?"

For a moment I thought that she meant her son. But then I understood.

"Alex?"

The name evoked no recognition in her eyes. "Alex went to America."

"To America?" she asked.

"Yes, he went to America."

"I know him," she said, this time referring to her son. "He will be back in a minute, you know. He doesn't know who you are or why I sent him away. He'll be back in five minutes, so I'll tell you what. Here is my address," and she scribbled it on the newspaper, "and my telephone number. Call me up; I would like to meet you." And as an afterthought, she asked: "Are you alone?"

"No", I said, "my wife and my son are here with me."

Quite mechanically, she inquired: "Is that your whole family?"

"No, I have a daughter too. She is in London."

"Well, I'm sure your wife will understand. I would very much like to talk to you. Let's meet, here or perhaps somewhere else."

I promised we would.

VIII

Ruth's group traveled to Naples. There they boarded a very old boat that chugged across the Mediterranean towards the shores of Palestine. Then they caught a glimpse of The Land, and there was excitement on board the ship, and then

166

... the British patrol boats appeared. Within sight of the Promised Land, their ship was diverted to Cyprus.

"The British," she said, "were now the new Gestapo of a new age."

They did not torture people in secret cellars. They did not tear out their hair or pull out their nails. They simply did not allow them to enter the Land that was their own.

So there they were in Cyprus, in yet another camp surrounded by barbed wire. True, they had food. They did not suffer any shortages. There was also adequate medical attention. But they were not free, still not free.

She understood that the British had a difficult job to do, caught between the two hostile camps, Arabs and Jews. Yet she felt it was totally inhuman to deny a people that had so recently come so close to total annihilation the right to enter their homeland.

While in Cyprus, she soon found out that she was carrying a new life in her body. During that summer night she had conceived a son whom, in due time, she had named Ezra. He was born in this internment camp.

Eventually world politics took yet another turn and she at last arrived in Israel, together with her son.

Then there was Gabriel, a man of about her own age, who paid attentions to her on the ship during the voyage to Palestine. He became her friend and companion and later her husband. Gabriel was a kind and considerate man. Not only did he understand the importance of that night, that fateful night with Alexander in Szombathely, but he was truly glad of it. He was glad that his wife-to-be had come to a new recognition of her womanhood so soon. So many others (he told her) still have not, and might never get there at all.

Gabriel wanted to have another son. It turned out to be a daughter. And then they tried for another son which, she said with a smile, also turned out to be a daughter. In time Alexander's son became truly Gabriel's. The boy never knew who his real father was.... Under the circumstances, an unimportant detail anyway.

Gabriel worked as a carpenter and made a good living, and Ruth came to admit that she loved him very, very much.

Yet that night, that fateful summer night, kept coming back again and again. After a while Gabriel did not want to hear about it any more. He said it was an old tale; it was done, finished with.

But for her it was not. Sometimes while she was walking along the streets of Jerusalem or doing her shopping or visiting some friends or accompanying her husband to synagogue, she would pray for the unknown man who had given that life to her. She often wondered what had happened to him. Had she given him more than a spark of life?

Then the Six Day War started. Nasser had threatened to throw the Jews into the sea, and Israel swung into a desperate counter-attack.

"Never again," said the land, said the trees, said the sea. "Never again! Never again shall we surrender to any threat or oppression. This time we shall fight. Then we could not fight them – those bustards, the fascists, the Nazis, - that was the last time in history."

Ruth's eyes were glowing with a new fire.

This time, if the world plays games with us, we will fight back, in a way that the world will never forget."

On the third day of the Six Day War Gabriel died a hero's death in the defense of Jerusalem, while advancing into the Old City. A sniper shot him, he fell, and it was all over.

Gabriel's death opened up great old wounds in Ruth. Now, again Ezra was left without a father. And as it had happened to many Jewish women throughout our history, it was left to her to bring up her children alone. She had loved Gabriel, but with his death that part of her life was now extinguished.

No, there were no other men. There probably never would be.

And then her question: "What did you say his name was?"

168

"Alex", I said.

She had written to the Red Cross. She had written to the Jewish community in Szombathely. But to no avail.

"Since you did not know his name, what did you say in your letters? How could you look for someone whose identity you could not discern?"

From a neat, tidy file she pulled out a copy of a letter and handed it to me.

"To the Rabbinate of Szombathely, Western Hungary:

This is an unusual request. In September 15th, 1945, I stayed in a flat at xxx in Szombathely. Apparently this flat was offered by the Jewish Community for use by transients who wanted to emigrate.

A young man who had also just returned from the camps was living next door to me at the same time.

This man still means a great deal to me. Please help me find him.

Yours,
Ruth xxx"

There was no response. Alex had vanished.

What was left for her were her children and the Land of Israel. Although getting on in years, she would still sacrifice her life for the country.

"If it came to that, we all would, you know. The Arabs are not our enemies. Our enemies are the ones who manipulate them from the background. For centuries we have lived with the Arabs in peace. You remember that the Golden Age of Judaism took place under the Moslems. We don't mind if they have their own country; in fact we would welcome it. But we will never again become the pawns of history."

Only then did I find out that Ruth was very active in Israeli politics.

So we had a nice talk, a quiet evening.

Later I met her daughters and her son. This time her son was polite and friendly. We talked about the world and politics and how things were in England, in America, in Canada, in Germany. There was no hatred in these young people against anyone. That impressed me. Ezra himself impressed me greatly.

After dinner the young man said: "You are not very far from where you are staying. Would you like me to walk you home?"

"Yes", I said, "I would love it if you came along." So we walked through the streets of Jerusalem. He told me of his beautiful childhood on the *kibbutz* where his mother and his father, Gabriel, had brought him up. In vivid colors he described the big garden and the trees and the fruit of those trees.

Ezra told me that he felt fearless, that all fear had been drained out of him. If it became necessary, and well it might, he would be willing to fight again, like his father had done, for Israel's victory. He would be willing to kill or be killed, if need be … but never again submit meekly to oppressors.

He did not intend to remain in the army permanently.

Although he was at a fairly mature age, Ezra wanted to study history. He yearned to become a historian and. was already taking some courses at the University. When his time in the Army would end, he would receive a pension. Then he could do what he liked. He could fulfill his dream.

He also wanted to travel around the world and see everything in order to put into perspective what he had learned about history.

"You know, Jancsi," he said, "I don't quite understand how you people" – that is how he put it, *'you people'* – "did not resist. I can never understand that."

I tried to explain. But then I thought better of it. I ought not to put doubts into his mind. Living in that tiny land, surrounded by millions and millions of Arabs waiting for the moment to attack, here was a young Jew who looked like an

170

Aryan god, who was fearless and compassionate, who had no real hatred in him, who wanted to study history and be a chronicler of his people, and who did not understand the Holocaust.

CHAPTER SEVEN

I

In 1978, in a large city in North America, I was invited to be the speaker, to recall my memories of the past, at an anniversary observance of the Warsaw Ghetto Uprising. This was one of the rare occasions when I addressed a very large audience about my experiences in the camps.

Nowadays when I speak in public, I may use the past as a part of the total human experience. My intention is to extend the implications beyond the purely Jewish framework to universal human applicability.

There were more than two thousand people in the audience. In a touching ceremony, six children lit six candles in memory of the six million martyrs, and a monument was unveiled in tribute to those who had perished at the hands of the barbarians.

As I was walking off the platform, a woman stopped me, put her hand on my shoulder and said: "You are Jancsi Heimler, aren't you?" I was somewhat taken aback by hearing the intimate name by which my family and closest friends call me. I searched for her face in my memory, but no recognition dawned. No, I was certain that I did not know this woman. How did she know my nickname?

"May I speak with you?"

"Of course," I said, yet I was wondering if the organizers of the meeting had some other agenda in mind. One of them, having overheard this little conversation, nodded. "You have ten minutes before the reception. And then we must drive you to the airport."

I went to a small room with this unknown woman. As we sat down, she immediately came to the point.

"I am the wife of Alex Benedict."

I visited Alex in his castle. Perhaps fortress would be a better word for it. It was large and rose high towards the sky. Wherever you looked there were stairs going nowhere. There were echoing dark corridors where at night ghosts floated through the dark. Time itself had been turned upside down; Alex moved in and out of different dimensions of reality.

He had been living in that castle for a number of years by then. When I entered, he could not tell whether I was a phantom of the night or of the day, or from beyond time altogether. But he spoke to me.

He felt that the enemy was down there. On the right hand side there was a large lake, or a river, or perhaps the ocean. Below the fortress the enemy was lurking, ready to attack at any time. The enemy wore uniforms. Sometimes the uniforms changed. But he saw them, and he knew that one day they would break through. So he had to escape, he had to run away from them, as far as possible. But from down below, the enemy was watching all the time. Day and night.

He saw it all. Day and night: His escape from the camp in Poland, then his arrest by the SS. There he stood, digging his own grave, amidst many other naked men and women. The SS man aimed his gun at him. A roar of explosion, and then he fell. He came to in darkness with the smell of blood all around him. Then he realized that he was alive. He began to crawl, pushing the dead bodies away from above him. Eventually he clawed his way out. He was naked. He ran. He saw a house. All he could remember later were the food, the smell of milk, the blanket around him, and an old peasant woman saying: "You cannot stay here."

He remembers he was dressed then and he was out in the night again. He ran. He ran towards the forest. And then he could not remember any more. Perhaps he fainted, perhaps he died, perhaps he came back to life. By the time the sun rose upon him, he was in the hands of the partisans. But perhaps he only dreamt the whole thing. He did not know.

In the castle, he saw it all. He saw himself raising his machine gun at dawn, just as the sun was rising. There they were, in their black uniforms. He stood alone; there were about fifteen of them. He killed them one after the other. He was not afraid. Afterwards he walked over to their dead bodies, looked each of them in the face and wondered, 'curious, they look like human beings!'

And now all these dead men were buried in the castle, and at night they came alive, came alive as ghosts. Now there was only one desire: There, somewhere in Poland or in Russia or wherever it was, to kill, to maim, to hurt, to inflict injury, to wipe out this black brigade until the last one of them was gone.

Now the ghosts were coming back at night. And he killed them again and again and again. Standing in the fortress he killed them.

He killed them.

The nights were long; images came from the past. He sat in school, a fire was burning; it was the fire of the crematoria burning the school.

One minute there was a cozy, warm atmosphere, the teacher was teaching them how to write. He saw the first letters taking shape in front of his eyes on the blackboard, but beyond it there was a fire and the crematoria was burning, - burning flesh. And he smelled the flesh and said to the teacher: "Teacher, they are burning, burning us." The teacher said: "Be quiet, Alex, be quiet. You are making too much noise."

And then he saw – did he see? Was he there? – the castle moving in time and space. He saw a field, a large, endless field. Dark clouds were gathering on the sky. He saw it all. The army came from all directions, with tanks and armored cars. They came. They wore other uniforms, they had a red star on their cap. He went with them, God only knew where. He went with them to kill, to rape, to kill. The dark secrets remained within him. Dachau, Buchenwald, Dachau, Buchenwald. Then Auschwitz, yes back to Auschwitz. And then the explosion, and then the grave, and then the forest, and then the Red Army, and women lying in front of him with their opened bodies begging, begging for life. And the rapes, and the nights and days. And his return. His return.

Now there was a moment of clarity, of lucidity. He said: "I tell you honestly that when I returned home, I forgot it all. I had really buried it in me. But now they are all here. I see those women, you see, I see them all. And the grave ... and the man aiming his gun at me. Death, life, resurrection, death, killing.

Jancsi, who am I? What have I done? What have they done to me?"

Before I could begin to speak, he said: "You are a Roman, or a Spaniard, are you? Are you? Have you also come here to finish me off, to tear apart the last vestige of my soul? Have you? Have you?"

He landed in New York. He saw the Statue of Liberty. Customs, immigration, names, documents, questions. "Yes," he replied to the immigration officer. "Yes, I was in a camp. Yes, I escaped. Yes, I have come here to live a life of freedom."

New York, 42nd Street. Dirt. People pushing. Holes, dark holes underground where naked men and women made love, drank and smoked. What did they smoke? God only knew; there was smoke in the air. And hopelessness. Despair, loneliness, a dirty room with a wash stand, and an outside toilet. Bugs at night. Bugs. Trying to learn the tongue, the language, the tongue, the language, the tongue, the tongue, the tongue. He put out his tongue and examined it as if in a mirror.

All this was encompassed within the fortress where Alex lived.

He sold real estate in New Jersey.

On commission. Was his commission ten percent, or twelve, or six? Commission.

A young man and woman bought a house. They looked Germanic, they should be killed. They ought to be killed. ...

And so it slowly began, slowly started, this dreadful, uncontrollable desire to kill, to maim, to hurt ... and to cry at night when he confronted his own soul.

He said to his soul: "Come, let us be reunited." And his soul said to him: "You cannot. You cannot. Never."

Walking the streets. Walking, walking in the rain, in the snow, in the cold. New York. An immense city where all the windows of the skyscrapers looked like blind eyes, not looking at him. Nobody was. The months passed and the years, and he was alone, alone, alone.

The George Washington Bridge. New Jersey. New York. New Jersey. New York. Manhattan. Dirty holes underground. Dirty women opening their thighs. Dirty, dirty, dirty. They should all be killed. Killed.

The doctor said: "You need help."

"Help? There is no help. The heaven is dark. The earth is dark. The cosmos is dark. The stars are dark. The universe is dark. Everything is dark. There is no help."

"You need help," said the doctor.

The streets. Brooklyn, the Bronx, walking, walking, walking. New Jersey, the George Washington Bridge, the Bronx, Madison Avenue, 42nd Street, Broadway. Neon lights. Movie houses. Alone. Alone. Always, always alone.

"Do you remember? Do you remember?" he asked when we saw each other for the last time. "Do you remember?" There was a flicker of recognition of something important in his eyes. Then it was gone. I saw the same expression in his eyes as I had seen in the eyes of *Gerhard Kaufman*. His soul was dead.

Dance halls. Something – an alien sensation, an alien feeling – said to him within his muscles, within his sinews, 'I want to love.'

He paid his money to the whore and she opened her legs. She should be killed.

The doctor said: "You should get some help."

Now they were all here. Everything was here in the fortress. And he was rushing up and down the invisible stairs that led nowhere and had no end.

"I am tired. Jancsi, I am tired, tired." Again he began. "Do you remember last time at home? Do you? Do you remember …"

Again his eyes glazed over. He could not see. All he could see were nightmares. The nights, the streets, Brooklyn and the Bronx and 42nd Street and crossing the George Washington Bridge to New Jersey and back.

Then a woman, Bertha, reached out towards him. The car, a kiss. A floating feeling of warmth. Marriage. Was it that? Was it marriage? What was it? What did marriage mean?

"M-a-r-r-..." he began to spell it.

"Jancsi, which side do you represent? Which side? Are you on the side of the dead or the living? What are you?

Bertha, Bertha. If that bloody bitch comes in here, I'll kill her, you know… I'll kill her. Me, children? Have children? Me. Not on your bloody life! Children are worms. They should be exterminated! Do you know that I was an SS man? Did you know that? Or – or was I killed? Yes, I was killed. They are all around there, down by the river, the lake, the ocean. They are there."

And he said: "Forgive them for they know not what they do. Who will forgive *me*? Who *could* forgive me? There is no God, only devils and ghosts and darkness."

Then he screamed: "Who are you? You bastard, who are you?"

I had to leave the castle, Alex's fortress, without having said a single word.

III

"Thus says the Lord God: Behold, O My people, I will open your graves, and cause you to come up out of your graves, and bring you into the land of Israel."

"And you shall know that I am the Lord, when I have opened your graves, O My people, and brought you up out of your graves."

"And I shall put My spirit in you and you shall live, and I shall place you in your own land: then shall you know that I the Lord have spoken it and performed it, says the Lord."
(Ezekiel 37, 12-14)

IV

Jerusalem. *Yad Vashem Holocaust Memorial.* Candles are flickering. An eternal light is burning in the middle of what looks like a cave. Children place flowers beside it, and the wall bears the names of Auschwitz, Birkenau, Dachau, Treblinka, Bergen-Belsen and other concentration camps. This is a memorial for the Six Million.

I stand there watching the flame. I want to be alone here for a while, but people are coming and going all the time. Someone is explaining to a group of schoolchildren what this all means.
To them it is history. To me, still a living reality.

I stand there watching the flame.
Father. I see him with his briefcase on his way to court. A portly man with graying hair, moving slowly down the steps of the staircase. I see him walking unhurriedly along the streets, greeting people and being greeted. A good man, perhaps a great man. He stood up against tyranny in 1918 and

again in 1938. He dared to speak out at times when only a few did. Now he walks towards the court. It is spring.

Then I see him in jail. Eva and I visit him, after the Hungarian police managed to get him out of the Gestapo's hands. They left his cell door open, so he can sit outside in the sun in the courtyard. The jail is just behind the court house to which he used to walk every day with his briefcase.

I see him smiling. It is a smile of encouragement which says, "I know I am finished. They will take me away. But you, the two of you, must stay alive." And he puts his hands upon our heads and gives us the ancient blessing of Israel. We leave. I never see him again.

Susan, my sister. I see her with her child Gabi in her arms. She is sitting on the balcony, looking down at the street. I shout up to her, "Is there anything to eat?" She smiles and gestures: "Come up!"

Susan. And Gabi, the little boy who had snuggled so deep into my heart.

Uncle Gyula. A stern man, straight as a ramrod, always walking erect like a soldier. He sells leather for shoes, boots, and other things. I see him standing in his shop. Through all my years of childhood I have never seen him smile. Perhaps he had no reason to smile. I don't know.

And Aunt Olga, his wife. Also stern, also unsmiling. Why don't these people ever smile?

And Miki, my first cousin and friend …

I see them and many more walking in procession past the flame at Yad Vashem. They had all walked into the fire. Yes, they were driven into it.

And what about me, who has survived? Where is my life going? Where am I going in my life? Where do I want to go? Where can I go?

Then it comes to me. Call it words, concepts, feelings, perhaps all of these together:

"It does not matter where you go. It does not matter what you do. It does not matter who you are. *What matters is that love is alive in you*. Ultimately that is all that counts. Do not be afraid of love and of loving. Most people are, you know.

Allow your love to grow like flowers in the spring. Allow your heart to be open, even if it is to pain. Only then will your heart be open to pleasure too.

Bring forth all that is hidden within you, do not be afraid. What is life if you are afraid to live the life granted to you?

Allow your dreams to become reality; do not be afraid of your dreams. Taste the spring and the summer and the autumn and the winter as intensely as you did when you were a child and everything around you seemed like a miracle. Taste it.

Now bury your dead, so that they may live on in you forever. You are back in the land from which once your ancestors started. The dream has been fulfilled. You do not have to spend the rest of your life bearing the burdens of the past. Not any more.

The world is in pain. Men and women are hiding from themselves. Give them a key. Help them to live. Open up the great concentration camp which is the world, and let there be joy and laughter and love and loving.

Teach people's hands how to touch and to feel. Don't let the skin become calloused by the insensitivity of our age.

Help men to see beyond the surface of things to the deepest core. It is a beautiful world.

Teach your children to open up themselves to what lies latent within them. Please try to teach it to others too.

But first and foremost bury, if you can, that which hurts. Then, perhaps, out of the deep soil a beautiful new plant will grow, perhaps a tree whose fruit will be sweet to the lips of men and women in this world.

Do not allow bitterness to become your master. Bury the bitterness too in the deep soil of the land. Let flowers and fruit spring forth from your bitterness.

And bury your hate, so that love may flourish and blossom and be felt by people all around.

180

That is the *message* which you must carry forth from *Yad Vashem*. You have not been destroyed. Your body may ache but your mind is alive, and the light within you – your soul – too. Go, and be a light. Do not be afraid. That is the only way to live."

…And the Great Old Man said to me:
"I have heard it all and, my friend, you are a Prince of Pain."
And I answered, "I am bearing the autumn now on my shoulders.
Life is all but gone. Whither now?"
And he said, "Go forth, my friend, and you will find
The bud of spring on your journey towards winter."
Then I said farewell and went my way.

Autumn sunshine lingered in the sky,
The flowers were closing shop for the winter,
Yet there was a small bud of hope in full bloom,
A memory of summer, of spring perhaps.

There was an ocean of tears in my eyes,
Frozen even under the burning sun,
And none to light a torch for
The great pain to abate.

And I walked dazed towards the winter,
Heavy with diamonds of ice,
And the bud beheld my frozen heart and felt
A purpose for her spring.

And she said, "Halt, my Prince –
I stayed alive for you to rest for a while.
The autumn is still yours, and my heart has still the warmth of spring
To melt your tears.

Please lie still in the pastures of autumn –
The fields are still alive with life."

And I lay on the fading grass
And thanked the bud for life and hope.
And my melting tears washed the pastures green.

V

Sunday, June 27th, 1976 was a hot day in Israel. Air France flight 139 *en route* from Tel Aviv to Paris left with 105 passengers on board. (men, women and children).

In Athens 56 new travelers joined the flight. The plane was airborne at 12.25 pm. At 12.33 pm terrorists hijacked the plane.

The Prime Minister of Israel, *Yitzhak Rabin,* was informed at 1.32 pm Israel time.

The evening edition of *Yediot Aharonot* announced: "Air France plane hijacked with scores of Israelis on it."

As an officer of the paratrooper, Ezra ben Gabriel took part in the rescue of the hostages at *Entebbe Airport* on the night of July 3rd, 1976, thus helping to enact one of the most heroic military rescue operations in human history.

By the next morning, exhausted and with his heart pounding, he was flying back with his comrades towards the rising sun, towards Israel. He knew what he had achieved.

Exactly thirty two years earlier, to the day, his father – wholly unknown to him –had been deported to Auschwitz. No one had said '*No!*' to the Nazi terrorists.

Now a new generation of Israelis, living as free members of their newly recreated nation, said '*No!*' at last. Ezra did not know his father, but he knew his people's history.

Some secret curse, he felt, had now been broken forever. The world could never play a cynical game with Jewish lives again; the arms of tiny Israel would reach anywhere.

As he sat in the plane, tears were rolling down his cheeks. Yes, the young soldier was weeping.

A few hours earlier he and his comrades had broken into the terminal building at *Entebbe Airport*, thousands of miles from Israel. Within seconds they had killed all the terrorists and freed the hostages.

His thoughts were racing fast, from his mother Ruth to his young wife whom he had left in his Tel Aviv apartment the night before, to his unborn child dreaming blissfully within his mother's womb. He thirsted for these people he loved so deeply.

Half asleep, he began to see images and pictures moving upon the screen of his mind.

He saw a small child walking at his father's side towards a mountain. He recognized that mountain; it was *Mount Moriah*. He himself was the child. He knew that something very strange was about to take place. Was it possible that this kind old man, his father, would hurt him? He sensed the conflict within the old man; he saw the tears, he heard the sighs. Then he saw the knife in his father's hand, and the glint of reflected sunshine. Then he heard a strange voice, a voice which came from nowhere and yet was everywhere …and the voice stopped it all.

And then, years later, as he looked down on his own young body and saw the foreskin missing from the flower of his manhood, he knew that he was bound to God forever and ever.

Other images came. *Masada*. As a grown man he was lifting the knife to kill his wife and daughter. And then, aiming at his own heart, he saw his body die and the soul of Israel living on...

Then he saw the great city of Rome. His mother's name was Lucillia, and he went with her to strange places in Egypt, and he grew up to be a man and he lived with monks on a hill overlooking a lake and he had children and the children had children of their own.

183

And centuries passed; and he, an old man, was a child again, this time in Spain; then in Russia, Holland and Germany.

And he faced the barrels of guns and there was a shot and he fell into a mass grave and soldiers in black uniforms stood around it. And they raised their arms to his death.

...The perennial recurrence of humiliation and murder was over at last. On this July 4th, 1976, a new sun was rising over Israel. No more mass suicide, no more graves, no more pawns in Christian history.

The soldier opened his eyes. He walked around the plane to visit the wounded. Then it was announced that they were about to touch down in the Land of Israel.

With pride, the captain announced, *"Mission accomplished!"*

At last, after two thousand years.

It is for the first time that a survivor has addressed himself to the descendents of his persecutors. It is for the first time that he opened his heart and allowed you to enter.

I hope, my young German friend, that you have allowed me to enter your life too and that the wall that separated us has fallen for ever.

Peace be with you, my young friend!

Yours,
Eugene Heimler

London – Calgary – Bermuda – London

EPILOGUE I

THE POWER OF HEALING

THE MEANING AND PURPOSE OF WORK

ENRICHING YOUR LIFE

The Jewish Sages saw the world as a polarity of opposites. The *yetzer ha-tov*, the good inclination, is juxtaposed with the *yetzer ha-rah*, the evil inclination.

Rabbi Nachman in the 3rd century A.C. was asked *"Is the evil inclination good?"* He replied: *"Were it not for the promptings of the yetzer ha-rah, no man would be inclined to build a house, or marry a woman, beget children or engage in business."*

To put it simply: without the negative there cannot be a positive. Without darkness there cannot be light. Without the interaction of positive and negative poles there can be no electric current or electric light. Energy does not stem from the positive alone but is the result of the tension between positive and negative.

If a man tries to deny the power of the negative within him, he will destroy himself and others.

Like the Therapeutae of Alexandria, I too believe that the power of healing is within us. But what do healing and power mean? How can I translate these concepts, so elusive in the abstract, into something useful and meaningful? My own struggles, ordeals, pains, depressions and illnesses have taught me that we do not listen well enough to what is going on within us.

We are not sufficiently aware of the *messages* sent to us through our bodies, minds and souls. We have been conditioned to obey the rules of the social order around us, so when the 'still small voice' begins to speak, we think there is something wrong with us. We tend to suppress this voice because it contradicts the clamor of society.

I remember that on the gates of *Auschwitz* and other concentration camps was written the inscription *"Arbeit macht frei"*, "work liberates". But work cannot by itself set anyone free, unless it is work freely chosen. Our occupations, the activities that take up half of our waking lives, are usually chosen at random, and so often turn out to be boring and soul-destroying.

Because we do not listen to ourselves, we are in no position to listen to others. We often cannot listen to our own children when they are trying to tell us what they would like to do with their lives. They might not be able to tell us in exact, explicit terms what they want to do, but by carefully observing even very small children we can clearly see their unique talents and originality.

Children demonstrate that the original condition of man is essentially a state of creativity. Then, because we are so conditioned, we proceed to teach them subjects such as mathematics and reading and writing and languages (which are indeed all of extreme importance). But unfortunately we tend to put more emphasis on the techniques of instruction and on producing results than in bringing the child's full range of abilities to fruition.

Near the end of our twentieth century, I believe it is no longer a luxury for people to devote their lives to what is satisfying and creative. We must rethink and redefine the concept of work so that everybody might do whatever he is equipped to do. We must once and for all resolve the condition of millions of people who are unemployed, in effect thrown onto the rubbish heap of society and made to feel that it is their own fault that they are unemployed. We are paying millions and millions of pounds, dollars and Deutschmarks in order to keep them unemployed, instead of using our immense financial resources to help them find an outlet which is useful to them as well as to the rest of society.

We are geared to a competitive society in which those who work are in competition with other workers elsewhere in order to survive. We have not given enough thought to an alternative order, one not based on competition but on cooperation. Large groups in our society, especially the aged and the sick, cannot afford to buy the expensive products of a competitive industrial system. Yet their needs are as great as those of others, maybe greater still. They too need shoes, and sometimes orthopedic shoes. They too need clothing and at times very special clothing because they feel the cold more acutely than younger or healthier people.

We have moved away from the idea of a compassionate society to that of an indifferent one in which everybody is looking out for himself. As a television advertisement puts it, "Looking after Number One."

Roman society in the age of Claudius Marcellus assigned very few duties to the privileged. Manual labor was performed by slaves. In his youth, busy exploring the pleasures of the senses, Claudius fell into a depression and suffered an inner hunger until he encountered a genuine community, some outstanding teachers and healers, who at last enabled him to find spiritual fulfillment. It was then that he discovered, perhaps not to his surprise at all, that he wanted to be a physician, a healer of others. Within the society in which he was born and brought up, this would probably never have occurred to him, because the basic, deep-rooted motivation would have been missing.

And so it is here in our own society as well. They say that there is no work available, that putting an end to unemployment is an impossible dream.

Among all ancient societies it was perhaps only in Judea that the dignity of work was recognized and accepted and, more remarkably still, work was based on a spiritual, religious foundation, as a principle of the Torah. Since slavery was abolished in Judea, work became the right and privilege of every free man.

187

In Israel it was deemed the duty of the free man to work with his hands. In the great Roman Empire of old, slaves did all needed labor, just as machines are doing our work for us today. In contrast, the Rabbinic Sages said: "He, who is productive and helps to get the world's work done, is a partner in God's labor of creation."

In ancient Israel and Judea, all those who were engaged in the teaching of the Torah were not allowed to receive any financial reward, nor would they have dreamed of accepting any. They were teachers, but they were also workers. *Rabbi Joseph* was a construction worker. *Rabbi Hoshea* was a laundryman. The great *Rabbi Hillel* was a wood chopper who sold his bundles in the streets of Jerusalem. *Rabbi Hilkiah* was a farm hand.

Jewish society expected its members to combine the study and teaching of Torah and Talmud with some worldly trade or occupation. Later on, during the Middle Ages, state and church authority alike were used to force Jews out of certain types of work and into occupations considered unworthy of Christians, such as tax collection and money lending. The Jews grieved deeply over the loss of their traditional trades and agriculture. Only in modern Israel has the Jew been able to rediscover and enjoy manual labor in all its diversity.

Now what does all this have to do with Yetzer ha-rah and Yetzer ha-tov? What have these things to do with healing and self-healing? Why was I so obsessed with the problem of the unemployed?

I do not consider work to be simply a means of making a living. It is the expression of the creative force within us. Therefore, in order to find this creative force, we must have very special ears to hear and very special eyes to see and a very special kind of sensitivity to perceive what a person from an early age might be able to do. More than that, I suggest that the real creativity of man lies within some unacceptable area of his life.

Usually we say to people around us that aggression is not acceptable. True enough. But aggression, if properly channeled and used, can make a man great in his own chosen field. I believe that surgeons at the operating table and lawyers in the courtroom are using their aggression in a very positive and creative way. And so are carpenters and electricians and mechanics and all others who enjoy their labor.

Now there are some people who, by the grace of God, find their own niche by working through and expressing the unacceptable. But not many. The great majority of men and women are bored with work. And this boredom infiltrates their personal lives too. So we have a generation of people who go through life marking time, waiting for it to end, yet unable to enjoy their free time either, because their boredom invades their leisure time too.

Work does not set man free unless he can freely choose his occupation.

We must find modern *Therapeutae* who will listen and hear, and who will help individuals explore their potential, not merely through tests and vocational guidance, but through internal discovery. We need *Therapeutae* that know how to see and feel another person, and enable him or her to express who he is and what he can do. These *healers* are needed to enable others to create their own paths and destinies.

The modern *Therapeutae* are to be combinations of healers, psychologists and teachers. But first and foremost they must heal themselves and live productive and enjoyable lives.

Children should be watched from the very beginning of their development; we must look out for their talents and potential.

And if at this stage of history creative work is not available to everybody, then we must create work, using national and perhaps international financial resources.

Men and women at present unemployed could still be useful to people with needs. They could work with their hands and with their hearts, and perhaps with both. We do not do that in our society. We have stopped hearing others. We only hear ourselves, and not even our own true selves that speak to us out of the depths, but the superficial self that merely repeats the slogans of the masses.

The *Therapeutae* must not only be healers of the soul but also practical persons who can channel the abilities of others into constructive frameworks.

I am of the modern *Therapeutae*.

I have become one for much the same reasons that, I think, my predecessors in Judea, Samaria, and in Egypt, had made such a choice. They found the world in a state of collapse. They found that values laid down thousands of years before had become hollow. People no longer heeded them. There were invasions and occupations. Brutal forces raped and ravaged nations. Long before Yehoshua/Jesus lived, the *Therapeutae* tried to revive ancient Jewish teachings, retreated into their communities and devoted themselves to their ideals.

My own primary task as an heir to the *Therapeutae* is not so much to heal the sick as to heal the healthy. My primary purpose is to allow people to see the overall pattern of their lives, so that they can choose what is worth living for. I have found some techniques to help people find real meaning in their existence. And not in labor and work alone, but in loving too.

Life without love and without work is not worth living. Even if they are born free, people without loving and working are slaves. I must tell you these things that I have learned in the course of my life, from my *Paraphant* and through Auschwitz.

I would like you to hear now an interview which I gave in Canada at one of the broadcasting stations. It might tell you a little more about my work.

190

INTERVIEW WITH MR DOUG GOSSEN
RADIO STATION CHFM IN CALGARY
February 12, 1980

G: Professor Heimler, shall we start by talking about some of your experiences that have led up to all this? First of all, how old were you when you went through these experiences in the Second World War?

H: *I was in my twenty second year. I was twenty two.*

G: And what kind of experiences did you go through? Can you tell us a couple of things that have happened to you?

H: *Well, Hungary was occupied by the Nazis in March 1944. First of all of course there was the great distress of the occupation itself, and the uncertainty of our fate. My father was a politician and he was very soon arrested.*

And then in July 1944 the deportation started from the Hungarian towns; I had lived in a small town in Hungary. I got to Auschwitz, the famous extermination camp, where millions of people have been killed. Knowing what was going on around you, - and sooner or later you had to know -, was an extraordinary, inexpressible experience: The knowledge that your own family and friends were actually dying; - the flames of the crematoria were really a kind of signal of death. Yet we did not know when, which night, they died. It was an incredible emotional experience. The extraordinary brutality of the SS and the Gestapo, the hunger and starvation, the physical pain caused by the beatings, all left a mark that will never go away. To sum up, the experiences were horrible. But the most horrible part of these experiences was that you had to close your mind's eye to what went on around you; because if you took everything in, then you just could not go on living.

The result of these experiences was that, long after they were over, they began to haunt me. Quite apart from the physical injuries which I received during the war, the psychological impact was much worse, and I had to cope with

191

that pain. My work is an outcome of all those camp experiences.

G: I gather then that the way you survived there was by shutting those experiences out of your mind. How long did you do that, before the memories started to come back?

H: *Well, you see, this shutting out is a very strange phenomenon. I understand it is known to psychology that if something is painful over a prolonged period of time, you simply don't acknowledge it. In my own case, I saw myself in third person singular: there he goes; there he is doing this, that or the other. I can tell you that I literally saw myself as if it wasn't me. This was one way of shutting out those occurrences. These experiences were not happening to me, but to him. It is a very well known syndrome in schizophrenia. So again I who had never shown any schizophrenic tendencies, - like so many other prisoners, - had to develop this kind of schizophrenic detachment.*

You ask how long it took before it began to register. Well, I would say that this, what I call survival syndrome or camp syndrome, took about ten or fifteen years before starting to creep back in dreams and in quite irrational fears.

I remember, I was walking along in London, when a little dog crossed the street. That was really the beginning of it. I broke out in a cold sweat, and I am not the kind of person who, after Auschwitz, is afraid of dogs. And yet ... it was totally irrational. And then it came to me, you know: There had been these huge Alsatian dogs with which the SS used to attack people. I had totally cut it out of my consciousness and now a little dog reminded me of it.

I had to feel very safe, in a safe democracy, I had to feel very safe with my wife (my second wife; my first wife had been killed in Auschwitz; my children were born in England), before nature as it were allowed me to confront this whole trauma. But as it began to come up, it was terrible. I call it my Second Auschwitz.

G: How did you manage to turn it around so that, now, it seems, you are using it in your favor?

H: *Yes, this is a very important and crucial question, not only in this interview but in my life, and to others who have survived, and perhaps to a new generation of people who may need to learn how to survive.*

How did I turn it around? Well, first of all, I went and tried to seek traditional psychiatric help. I had psychoanalysis. It helped me a lot. I had it five times a week at a very famous clinic in London. It helped me to understand some connections between the past and the present.

Where it did not help was that neither the analyst nor I could begin to understand the sheer magnitude of what had happened. You see, the experiences that I was recalling had been real. Never in her life had my analyst come across anything like that. So at the end of it, though I could work and study, I was left with very, very serious problems. And when such episodes as the one with the little dog for instance, began to happen, I was afraid to go anywhere where there were a lot of people.

Now my job involves meeting people, addressing people. I have been teaching at London University; I have done so for twenty years. Imagine going into a classroom and being afraid! And not knowing what you're afraid of, breaking out in a cold sweat, heart pumping 140 – 150 a minute. These were all experiences that first of all had to be understood.

I literally sat down with a tape recorder and talked into it in desperation, since there was nobody who could understand. As I listened back to what I had been saying, the memories started to flood back. Then I said to myself, all right, it is no use asking questions like 'Why did these things happen?' I would never get an answer. For my own sanity's sake I must try to do anything, even the impossible. Yet, what could I do?

I don't want to be melodramatic, but as soon as I asked this, answers from within my own experiences began to come. I heard the advice come from within myself:

'You need to go inside the very situation of which you are most afraid, and be prepared for what you are afraid of.' As I

began to go inside, it turned out that overcoming this kind of fear added to my experience of something positive, and resulted in my victory over the horror.

Eventually my performance at work improved. The anticipation of fear was totally gone. Eventually I began to use my so-called negative feelings like aggression and hate. After all, I mean, if someone goes through something like what I have gone through, it would be inhuman not to feel hate or aggression. But I knew that if I were to express these feelings just as they were, I would end up in prison again. So I had to find an acceptable alternative expression.

One of my outlets was to write. I find that in writing I can express those feelings. A creative structure is extraordinarily helpful. Then I began to understand something else.

Why are people like some surgeons or lawyers – my own son is a barrister in London – good at their professions? Because they can use in a positive way what society considers being negative. And the trouble is with those people who cannot find a niche in society where they might use such potential.

So that is how I coped with it: first by going into the situation, and then by finding out how I might use the unacceptable in an acceptable way.

How did I get to teach this, and why am I here in Calgary part of each year?

The answer is this: Through this interplay of positive and negative I came upon a new philosophy of life and living which is valid for me and, I believe, can be so for others too. But it is also a system, a scientifically validated system, of looking at people's disadvantages (what they regard as their disadvantages) and trying to turn these into assets.

G: You went through something that was horrible beyond what anyone of us can even imagine. Yet you feel that this can apply to others, to us. Such extreme things don't have to happen to us. We can apply it in situations that we consider terrible, though they really might be very, very minor compared to what you underwent.

H: *Any pain, physical or emotional, whether it happens to people here in Calgary or Edmonton, or anywhere else in Canada or England or beyond, is their own Auschwitz. You cannot compare it in terms of degrees. A threat against one's life in Calgary is just as grave as a threat against one's life in some dramatic place like Buchenwald. Yes, I am saying that anyone, anywhere, with some professional help or guidance, can learn to structure and use what is usually called negative.*

For a long time we have been trying to get rid of the supposedly unacceptable feelings within us. I feel that this is not right. What we must do is use what we have rather than get rid of it.

By analogy, in the case of electricity it would be ridiculous to say to the negative pole: 'Go away!' The moment you cut it out, you get a short-circuit. And what applies to the law of energy in nature applies equally to the law of energy in man. My system, if I might call it that, my way of looking at people and at myself is to use what we have, rather than analyze it away.

I don't say that this is one hundred percent successful – I don't know of any model that is one hundred percent successful -, but I would say that in sixty to sixty-five percent of cases where people have problems - and they don't have to be psychiatric problems -, they would succeed provided that they are willing to go through hell before finding the key to heaven. And this is very difficult.

G: That's interesting. As you put it, you went through all this, and after everything that you did, and the follow-up to it, you came up with a philosophy, or found an actual way to go beyond philosophy that is very practical. I wonder if we might talk about that for a moment: the *Heimler Scale of Social Functioning*. Do you apply that sort of philosophy or way of thinking in a practical way, such as a series of questions, in order to analyze someone?

H: *Well, it seems to be the opposite. Instead of analyzing people it tries to put them together again. Like Humpty Dumpty. The questions aim at getting answers to basic areas of life. They are very simple questions, like 'Do you like the work you are doing?' To this particular question there are three possible answers. Either you do, which is 'yes'; or you are not sure, which is 'perhaps'; or 'no'. But as I ask these questions of you, I do not know what the experiential meaning is behind the answer, whatever that answer might be. So I can hand the Scale back to you and ask you 'Well, you said 'yes', or 'perhaps' or whatever, what do you mean by that?' Many people who find it difficult to think in abstract terms open up because they have something concrete in front of them.*

Or take another question, this time about finances. 'Do you feel safe or secure about spending money?' Now the person gives whatever answer he does, one of the three possible alternatives. Then you again turn to him and ask, 'Can you give me an example, or examples?' Immediately some kind of communication begins.

So the Scale is, in one sense, a means of removing the barriers to communication between two people. One of them is skilled in interviewing, whether he or she is a priest, a clergyman, a social worker, doctor, nurse or teacher.

Then there is another use to this Scale, too. The answers can be computed into numbers, and through this particular computation you can find the levels on which people function. You add up the answers, you add up on the one side what is satisfying, and you add up on the other side what is frustrating

Say out of a possible maximum of 100 % on the satisfaction index you score 70 %, and on the frustration index you score 30 %. Research proves that that is fine, that represents a balance. But if, say, you score 30 % on the satisfaction index and 70 % on the frustration index, something is wrong. It isn't I who say that there is something wrong with you, but you yourself are saying it. We can then identify the areas that are open to change, that can be transformed.

So the Scale is useful for evaluation or, to use a medical term, in diagnosis. But beyond that it is useful in that it

196

enables us to predict. The mass of data we have accumulated enables us to see emerging patterns and to predict future potential problems.

For example, we know that people whose satisfaction rates are dropping – say, young people out of a job – at a certain point may commit crimes. This we know, not from thin air and mere speculation, but from statistical evidence. Dropping out of society is, for some people, not merely a matter of withdrawal into themselves but turning against society.

Probation officers in Britain (many of whom have been trained in this approach) will tell you that when satisfaction scores are dropping and frustration scores increase, within a very short space of time the person is likely to commit criminal acts. In some other situations a similar pattern of events might lead to illness. And I don't mean necessarily mental illness: for reasons which we do not clearly understand, it is often also physical illness.

What I am teaching my students here in Calgary and in other places, in Germany, America, Holland and Britain, is based, perhaps for the first time, on mathematical computation and is designed to lead to an accurate assessment of forecast about a human situation.

G: How has this been accepted by people in the medical professions, or in the legal profession, or in the judicial system?

H: *Initially it has had a rough ride. People will doubt and question anything that is unusual or novel. The least skeptical of all were the medical people. Almost all my articles have been initially printed in medical journals. I suppose this is because physicians are used to scientific thinking; they were the first ones to be really helpful. The original help in Britain came from the Medical Research Council. So I have had very, very few problems with the medical profession.*

Many more problems came from people like psychologists and social workers whose jobs involve testing. Social workers less so. As for the psychologists, I suppose they didn't like the idea that a non-psychologist was creating something.

If you ask me where we stand today, after some 16 or 17 years of its existence, ten years in a teachable form, I would say that the scientific basis of the system is by now unassailable. The research is so vast and comes from so many respectable places - hospitals, clinics, universities in so many countries -, that it is pretty well established.

You asked about the legal profession. They are involved only indirectly, through the probation service. It is extremely popular among probation officers in Europe, especially in Germany and England.

What I am awfully concerned about is that this tool of evaluation should not be regarded in Court as a final assessment. It would be terribly dangerous if people were assessed on the basis of a piece of paper, with answers on it. What I want, and what I teach - and I believe judges and magistrates are attuned to this approach -, is that people might refer to the content of the Scale, yet the jury and judge or magistrate must make up their minds as to the facts without any influence from the scientific data.

I am very careful, and therefore I keep tight control over the registration of people who do this kind of evaluation. I would never accept it if anyone could go to court and say: 'The Scale says so-and-so, and therefore this man is going to commit a crime, and therefore he should go to prison.' Nor would the legal system accept that; it would be frightening. But to say, 'My Lord, this man is in great pain, for such and such reasons, and I know this from my interview with my client', without even mentioning that this information is based on a piece of paper called Scale of Social Functioning – yes, that makes sense.

G: Do you, then, maintain control over it? Do you have some type of copyright as to who may use it?

H: *Yes.*

G: How do you maintain that?

198

H: Well, 100 % safeguards do not exist. But there is an international copyright agreement, and anyone trained through the University gets a contract or registration. Originally this was directly through me; now it goes through either the University or the appropriate body in the particular country or location. The copyright is connected with safeguards for training. I am quite sure that there are breaches of the copyright. But it is difficult to lawfully use this system without training. Yes, it can be misused.

There was an instance in Kent, in England, where somebody, though trained but not trained properly, or trained a very, very long time ago, used it and published it. He did have the right to use it, but he was not up to date. Other probation officers attacked him for the inadequate use of the Scale, to the point where an apology was printed in 'The Justice of the Peace' – the journal for probation officers and judges – apologizing to me for this breach of copyright.

So the control is not by me but by all the other people who have been trained and who will watch very carefully that adequate protection is given to safeguard this system.

G: Has this been good for you financially?

H: I don't think I get a hell of a lot financially from the Scale, you know. If I were cleverer or commercially minded, I could have made a fortune. I think that selling Scales and having a copyright doesn't bring you a fortune when you are busy training students and people in the helping professions. No. It brought in something but not much.

G: If you had been aggressive about it, you might have made a fortune. Were you ever tempted to do something like that? It sounds like the type of thing – especially during the last few years when everybody is concerned with self-examination through biorhythm and astrological charts-, which might fit into this kind of area. Wouldn't somebody try to exploit it in that way?

H: Well, in the United States some people have tried to – not only tried to but actually published the Scale –, sometimes with and sometimes without my permission. But these were very respectable scientific and medical people. But the kind of commercialism that you mentioned I would not do. It will not happen in my lifetime and if it remains in my family it will not happen, not legally anyway.

You don't go through the kind of experiences I went through in order to make a fortune. This may sound a little bit idealistic, but then you have to account not only to yourself but to the six million dead too. If I went all out for money, it would make my situation very difficult. I do not say that I don't welcome the invitations I receive from all over the world, including Canada. I cannot complain that I m not earning enough. What I am saying is this: I am not selling my soul to the devil.

G: One more question: What about the future use of it? Are you, through interviews like this, publicizing it more widely so that it would be more widely accepted or used? Would you like to see that happen?

H: *I am very ambivalent about this, you see. I don't really think that interviews of this kind do much publicity for the method, because in the final analysis it must be learnt at a proper place such as a hospital or a university. All that people listening to this can really do is contact agencies if they themselves need help or want to clarify some issues. That, for example, can be done through the University of Calgary at the Faculty of Social Welfare, or in other places at similar establishments.*

I don't think that I do this kind of interview for the sake of publicity, either for myself or for my system, but rather in order to give some struggling people hope that overwhelming problems can be changed into assets. I myself have had such problems and sometimes I have them still. I know that frustration is really the potential for satisfaction.

This kind of program should make people aware that there is hope, that they need not see things in black and white. I stopped selling ideas a long time ago. Since I stopped doing that, everything goes much better.

G: Great. Thank you very much. As a matter of fact, we have just run out of tape.

I have told you a great deal about my early life, my young German friend, about my parents, about the town where I was brought up as a child. I have told you about my early experiences as a Jew, how I grew up carrying within me an invisible curse. I have made references to my work which takes me to Germany and to other lands. I have let you read a conversation with a Canadian radio reporter.

At this juncture I can tell you something about this wandering Jew, who travels around the world selling a survival kit called *"Human Social Functioning"*.

If I say too little, I cannot really convey to you how I translated the past into my current personal and professional life. Creative Listening, as I tried to convey, is a very important part of my work. By that I do not mean mere listening with boredom, or while preoccupied with my own thoughts, or thinking of answers, clever or otherwise, that I might give to the people who need me. The kind of creative listening that I am talking about is difficult to learn.

I am a listener who listens with what Theodor Reich described as "Listening with the Third Ear."

Surely listening is not a fulltime job. Perhaps, though, it ought to be, especially in our day and age, when no one listens to anyone any more. We are so full of the need to talk that we have not trained our ears to perceive the *messages* sent out by others, the *messages* that come from within, from our mind, our body and our soul.

Throughout my life I have learned how much freedom really means to me and to all those who are alive.

Freedom is not a mere slogan but a factual state. It means that, if I so wished, I could take my passport right now, this afternoon or evening, and fly to Brazil. It means that if

201

someone confronted me with ideas or thoughts with which I did not agree, I could say so without arrogance, aggression or apology.

There will be no secret police watching my thoughts or actions, no jail, no torture, no persecution. I can say these things without fear or dire consequences. I can utter my convictions confidently and though you or others might not share them, there will be no ominous consequences.

Freedom means to me that I can respect myself for what I am, and respect you for what you are. That no government, politician, *Führer* or dictator can tell me what and when and how I should think, or how I must feel.

I am writing this book by dictating it into a tape recorder; it will be transcribed and translated in West Berlin. I don't have to be concerned that a censor might come and say: "We have to cut out this bit; that bit won't do." There will be no knock on my door at three o'clock in the morning to say, "Eugene Heimler, you have said things which go against the State, or the Party, or whatever."

So I learned in my life that what is most important for a man is to feel free and to be free. I know that absolute freedom does not exist and perhaps cannot exist if we are to live together as a community.

But ... this freedom is perhaps the basic aspect of my work: allowing people to speak; to say whatever is on their minds. I am neither judge, nor jury, nor advocate, but a fellow human being who is there, first of all, to hear. After hearing, my task is to try to reflect back, not the mere words, but the meaning of what I have heard, to the one addressing me.

What for? A good question.

I believe that our upbringing from our earliest years in effect estranges us from our own selves. My generation, and in a way yours too, never learned to discern what is right for us and what is wrong for us. We were simply told what was right or wrong. And I believe that the voices of parents, uncles, teachers, of a whole warped society, are still reverberating within us to a point where none of us can say '*I*'

202

any more. Consequently, we cannot say 'you' any more, either.

Of course I am not saying that the education of children is unimportant, that there should be no guidelines and basic laws regulating society, that there is no right and wrong. What I am saying is that nowadays we do not allow the child to find the man within himself, or the woman, for that matter. So often the word 'I' is heard – *"I want"*, *"I need"*, *I, I, I, me, me*. A whole generation is screaming over its deafening music into the world: *"Listen to me, me, me!"*

Yet those who have found the *'I'* or the *'me'* within themselves have no need to shout. Having found their own identity, they are able to use it for themselves and for others.

We are still living in an age in which there are great dangers of being told who we are and what we should be. Millions of people all over the world never find their identity. So they go to work. What for? Work gives them neither fulfillment nor pleasure. They still cannot allow their feelings towards others to be open, frank, and free from arrogance or aggression.

We live in a world in which people must find the *'I'* in order to find the *'you'*.

After I came out of the camps, my great turmoil, vast depression and anxiety did not overwhelm me immediately. They took many years to come to full sway. With paper (and later on, a tape recorder) in front of me, I sat down and poured out all the things that I felt were relevant to my life. As I read back or listened back what I had been saying about my current miseries, the past flashed back in vivid colors.

Gradually, not at once, a bridge was forged between the then and the now. As I began to walk backwards and forwards on this bridge, I slowly discovered that I had a right to be who I was. This right applied to many areas of my life that had been hidden before, including those that I felt uneasy or guilty about.

Most people have the idea or thought that there is something wrong with them. The Christian tradition speaks of sin. Peoples' minds are weighed down by supposedly sinful thoughts that they regard as unacceptable to themselves or others or society as a whole. Hitherto psychotherapy followed in the footsteps of the Christian tradition that one must understand their 'negative' feelings. With the assistance of a good therapist, having understood their feelings, each person must resolve them. It was taken for granted that those 'sinful thoughts' needed resolution, needed to be gotten rid of.

Just as in days of old people needed to drive away the *devil* or torture those possessed by the *devil*. The truth is that, if there is a *devil* in man, he is there for a good reason. The *devil* is only there for the time being, until his useful purpose in people's ordinary lives can be found.

The issue is thus not how we might chase away that which is unacceptable within us. You can't chase away the negative polarity in electricity. Rather we need to find ways and means in reality, in action, to enable the apparently unacceptable to become acceptable, and thus to nurture our human growth.

Freedom thus means not simply concepts and ideas but deep-rooted feelings that await expression. At first the expression may be in words. And then the feelings which have expressed themselves verbally need to be translated into some acceptable reality. This new reality will help the individual (or individuals) to grow and will enrich society by rendering it more colorful and varied, without harming anyone.

Human Social Functioning is a process of listening in order to help people channel their unacceptable feelings, wishes and desires into acceptable ones.

In daylight nightmares disappear. What looks like a nightmare in the dark can be beautiful in the sunshine.

Man needs to have the freedom not to be afraid of himself. People afraid of themselves are afraid of others. Frightened people hurt others or themselves. Frightened nations hurt each other too. This idea is by no means the whole of my system. But it is its core.

To be means taking the risk to explore. And having explored, taking the action to fulfill one's destiny.

These concepts I have just discussed are the most important principles of my work.

Let me give you just one example:

There was a man in London, a lawyer by profession, who had left his job and was totally at a loss. From morning to night, with a half lost memory, he sat in striptease theatres, looking at the gyrations of naked women and feeling, for reasons he could not understand, very guilty about what he was doing.

The exposure of naked flesh, however, gave him no satisfaction; the women were distant and unattainable.

He could not work; his mind was partly gone.

One day he somehow found his way to me and we began to talk. I mirrored back to him what he was saying, helping him to see himself as he really was.

He had hoped that I would remove this evil from him, because he considered the wish to watch these naked women as a grave and terrible weakness.

But I did not try to eradicate what he considered his big flaw. He was very surprised that I helped him to think in terms of how he might use this guilt, shame and desire for his own good, instead of trying to talk him out of it.

I did not analyze its roots, why and how it all came about, but rather tried to establish that it was there, and what he might do in order to connect this to the reality of his life without shame, but rather with genuine creativity.

And so it came about that, after we had explored various possibilities, he studied and became a fashion photographer.

Now, through the camera, he could use his gift. At first he photographed half-naked women; later, properly dressed ones. In the course of his new work he met a model, who became his wife. At close quarters and in close contact with her he could live out what was before mere fantasy. What had been at one time a feeling of utter defeat became an awareness of triumph.

Today I can report that this man is one of the most outstanding and acclaimed fashion photographers in England.

Thus what I have been talking about with Eleazar ben Yair concerning the unemployed and what I was trying to do with them essentially boiled down to this:

Ideas and thoughts that are unacceptable at one point in time can become acceptable at another. We must shape them and structure them, not try to talk them out or away, but learning to use them for the benefit of ourselves and others.

You have witnessed a radio interview in Canada, which touches upon some of my work with people which enables them to live fuller, richer, more creative lives. You have also seen how the past, for instance my dialogue with Eleazar ben Yair about my work, has enormous relevance to me. My work with unemployed people confronted what at that time was a very major problem in Britain and, as a matter of fact, what to this very day represents a growing affliction all over the Western world.

POSSIBILITIES OF TREATMENT
OUTSIDE PSYCHIATRIC HOSPITALS

Address delivered at the Conference of the World Health
Organization,
sponsored by the World Federation for Mental Health, the
International Hospital Federation, Belgian Ministry of Health and
the State University of Ghent, Belgium,
At Ghent on March 31st, 1980

"Increasing numbers of people in the community are
facing uncertainty and a feeling of insecurity regarding their
functions, prospects and abilities to exist in society.
Unemployment, inflation, the energy crisis, together with fast
and vast technological developments demand continuous
changes from those still in the workforce, thus causing
economic and industrial unrest which at times threatens the
established institutions and traditional democracy.

Individuals caught up in these changes experience
increasing frustrations in their lives, with resultant tensions
and anxiety. They feel helpless to overcome the external and
internal stresses and often find escape routs in alcohol, in
somatic and psychosomatic symptoms and syndromes, which
consequently may lead to dependence on drugs of various
descriptions.

In plain language, more and more people "break down",
carry the burden of their condition outside the walls of
hospitals, and demand ever increasing support from
physicians and supportive agencies. They might occasionally
need short-term admission to hospitals, only to return
thereafter to the world of high voltage stress, and so the
vicious cycle continues.

Our traditional thinking is based on a model of illness and
health. We regard people who cannot function within the
social system as ill. This needs to be re-examined in the light
of the causal factors operating in the modern industrial world.

If health is the norm, we must define what that means,
and not only in terms of the absence of symptoms. But if the

207

majority of people is frustrated, ill, unhappy, empty (or whatever other term we may use for non-functioning or difficulties in functioning), and if this is seen as the norm, then we must shift from the traditional medical model (illness/health) to something new, or at least different.

That unhappiness is the root of many psychological and psychiatric conditions, is well known. These conditions however are often a result, not the cause. If then we need to offer treatment, care, guidance, primary care or whatever else to people in need, outside of hospitals, within an emerging new model of care, then this will have to have its own discipline, methodology, philosophy and techniques, with a strong bridge to the medical profession.

I will therefore use the term 'facilitating care' to denote treatment within this new, emerging modality.

While the medical model must be maintained for those who need admission to hospitals, the new model needs psycho-social educators and facilitators, rather than therapists in the traditional sense. Paradoxically, if the majority of people in our society, both the employed and the unemployed, are feeling empty, frustrated, depressed and anxious, then the terms "treatment" and "therapy" are no longer applicable.

Three aspects of what I call 'facilitating care' need to be described.
1. Who needs such care?
2. How to provide it?
3. What are some of the methods and techniques required for use in the community, outside the hospital walls?

Ever more young men and women leave school fearful of being thrown onto the rubbish heap of society. They know that they don't have the slightest chance of gaining any sustained employment or of using their abilities in any productive way. At best, they can look forward to being kept by the State for the rest of their lives.

208

Abundant evidence shows that human beings, from earliest childhood onwards, want to explore, express and share their abilities with others. Child guidance in the early days has shown that when the child begins to express himself and communicates through play, the therapist has a fighting chance, even with disturbed children, to help them heal.

Play may or may not be preparation for life and work, but it is certainly an expression of a need to explore and to communicate. Clinical observations show that some psychotic children cannot play. What happens to a young adult who is denied the possibility of exploration and useful expression? We see the answer in increasing violence against persons and property, in addictions of all kinds, and in the inability to build lasting relationships.

The immense energy locked up in the young can be released and channeled into creative use, whether in work or in other life tasks. If we could redirect the financial resources of public assistance for the able-bodied young so as to help explore their real abilities for some meaningful life-tasks, then we might re-channel and redirect their energies towards productive purposes, to the benefit of themselves as well as of society. Such a life-task – and this is the only way in which it would differ from 'work' in the usual sense – would not be part of the competitive economic system.

To whom, then, will these young men and women offer their skilled services as, say, shoemakers, carpenters or plumbers? Before answering the question, I must once again emphasize that I am speaking of two distinct kinds of redirection:

1. The redirection of financial resources at present known as public assistance and welfare and social security, so as to enable the young to receive training and wages; and

2. The redirection of the energies of the young, through imaginative exploration of their abilities, starting in school.

Who will be the recipients, the beneficiaries of their productive efforts?

There are two groups in the community who, in addition to human contact, need material assistance: the aged and the physically handicapped. An old couple may have many needs yet lack the money to meet these: orthopedic shoes, repairs to the leaking roof, blocked drains, electrical repairs, and many more. They may not be able to pay the full costs, but could certainly contribute a reasonable share. The rest would be subsidized.

My own work over the past 25 years with the unemployed (including the young unemployed) has shown how meaningful activity can turn destructiveness into constructive conduct. I believe that, with proper financial management and economic distribution of the available resources, new kinds of cottage industry and workshops could be created, and wages paid which would match the trade union rates paid for similar work in the competitive arena. As far as the public is concerned, such workshops and industries would be indistinguishable from any other, and free from any stigma of inferiority.

Governments already subsidize nationally useful industries. The British Government has been doing so for some time, and the work force has certainly not regarded this as a gift of charity.

I believe that the Trade Union Movement would not object, but welcome the emergence of such a life-task force. It would pose no threat to existing jobs at all, because the needy groups in society can seldom if ever afford to call upon the services of the competitive economic arena. Sooner or later, most members of the Trade Union Movement itself would become, if for no other reason than because of their own retirement, beneficiaries of the life-task force.

The actual management and distribution of funds may or may not be done by Governments. There is a tradition in Britain and in Holland, for example, that important ventures of this kind are channeled through voluntary organizations.

Personally, I would welcome this latter alternative, as by nature and past experience I tend to suspect power and government authority. I would hate to see members of the life-task force become civil servants. Rather, in a caring society, they would to be true servants of the aged and the sick.

Yet another group who will need the life-task force consists of men and women who lose their jobs. Some may want to offer their acquired skills and know-how to this new communal service, rather than face a prolonged interruption of activity.

Unemployment, and the inability to carry on useful activities, often brings about depression, anxiety, and increasing strains in family and marriage relationships. Whether participation in the life-task force is a temporary or a permanent solution does not really matter, as long as the continuity of activity is maintained. My reference to the possibility that the life-task force may be of a temporary nature indicates that I see a bridge between the supported and the unsupported, between the subsidized and the unsubsidized arenas of activity.

The third group is well known to most people in the helping professions. These are individuals who find their work so frustrating or demoralizing that they move into "internal emigration". Many stress symptoms, among them repeated absenteeism and frequent hospital admissions, appear among this group. Treatment alone may not be enough if, on return, they face the same environment of work which originally contributed to their breakdown. Usually these people are middle-aged and can often see no way out of their predicament. A thorough exploration of their real abilities, together with an opportunity to put their newly found life-task into practice, might change their mood into one of optimism and hope.

Finally, people who are discharged from hospital after long and chronic illness need, in addition to thorough after-care, an opportunity to be useful.

211

Every study I have undertaken, every research I know of, convinces me that human beings who feel useless will become destructive or self-destructive in time. Conversely, those who feel useful, even the retarded, can be constructive to an amazing degree.

Thirty years in England have taught me not to expose my personal life to strangers, to be wary of overstatements, and not to display great emotions. I apologize for having now to break the unwritten rules of my adopted country, at least as far as my personal life is concerned. About emotions I shall be more careful, though my Hungarian heritage may break through here and there. As this is mainly Continental audience, perhaps I shall be forgiven.

In the summer of 1944 I found myself in some Nazi extermination camps, including Auschwitz and Buchenwald. There were some outer camps under the umbrella (if that is the right expression) of Buchenwald, among these was a camp called Troeglitz. Here, during August 1944, the SS commandant embarked on a "mental health experiment" to establish how useless and purposeless work would undermine the prisoners' will to live, and to "measure" how many would actually commit suicide. From the SS point of view, the experiment proved to be highly successful. We were ordered to carry sand and rubble from one end of the compound to the other, some four miles' distance, and then carry it back again. Within a few days "results" began to accrue. Some of my companions, mainly middle-aged men, simply gave up and died. Others ran against the electrified wire fence which surrounded the camp, thus committing suicide. Many more became psychotic.

This crucial episode laid the foundations for my ongoing interest in the unemployed and in the importance that purposeful, meaningful activity has for people. I have pursued these areas in various professional capacities, through research and practice, ever since.

After the war in England, I worked with a great many unemployed men and women, and took careful notice of their lives and struggles. It was then that I began to search for some commonality amongst this group of people, in order to ascertain where and how I could assist those most.

As time went on it became ever clearer that whether unemployment was the cause or the result of their troubles, almost all of them were carrying a burden from which they could not free themselves.

But unemployment is but the visible tip of the iceberg. The real burden of our present human condition is that many of us do not know our own inner resources or the way towards finding out about them. A great deal of suffering in our lives is due to our inability to use ourselves. Such blockages, over prolonged periods of time, created cumulative frustrations, with resulting ills of all kinds

By the end of the '50's I have had access to some 1200 such men and women. Their embitterment not only produced often serious clinical symptoms but also permanent personality changes. Once they had reached this point, they were increasingly unable to accept the help offered to them. A definite relationship manifested itself between massive, prolonged frustration and the inability to function within society.

I spoke about 'facilitating care'. I ought to define how this can help people find meaning and purpose for their existence outside hospitals, in the community. Man's modern crisis is an existential vacuum which must be filled if we are to prevent a collapse of our society. Modern industrial life, with its strains and stresses, is creating a "Mental Health Experiment" akin to what the Nazis did with us during the summer of 1944. This time, however, we are not helpless.

Necessity is the mother of invention. Those men and women in England were so hypnotized by their own troubles that they could see nothing else. How could I show them that beyond the tree that was blocking their vision, there was a whole forest of life – of rich and hopeful life? How could I convince them that their current predicament might only be temporary, if only they would accompany me on a journey of self-discovery?

In that setting of a Local Authority Health Department, words and interpretations were of very little worth. The limiting time factor also presented a problem. So necessity led me into an area in which I had no previous training or know-how.

A series of questions kept recurring. I wrote them down and, in due time, selected and organized these recurring central themes. Soon enough I formulated some kind of instrument which concerned itself with the vital areas of life: work, finances, social relationships, family life (past and present), and the more personal areas (which included sexuality). As you will notice, these are no more than chapter headings in a social history.

After eliminating many others, I articulated each area into five questions. So, by the mid fifties I had a list of 25 such questions. They were sufficiently open-ended to allow my clients to indulge free association, yet precise enough to permit a very simple scoring system. Each question could be answered with "yes", "perhaps" and "no", bearing the arbitrary numerical values of 4, 2, and 0 respectively. Thus each area could carry a maximum of 20 points. At that time, the instrument (or call it what you will) had the maximum total or 100. It had to be simple because adding up figures had never been my strong point.

I then began to do two interlinked processes. First, I would hand them back the paper after they had answered the questions and would ask them to explain to me the experiential significance that lay behind their answers. To my surprise I found that even clients who were not very talkative began to spell out what those answers meant to them. Again to my great surprise, they then proceeded to connect various answers with one another. Now it appeared that I could also score an overall 'satisfaction index' to see how much (or how little) total satisfaction they have had in their lives. I also used my information to communicate my so called 'findings' with them. Once again, this met with much appreciation from them.

Almost a decade later, I began to look for a pattern: how does the absence of satisfaction manifest itself in clinical symptoms? This too was structured into five areas: activity (in those days I called it 'paralysis of activity'); somatic or psychosomatic syndromes; feelings of persecution; and finally, various escape routes, such as drugs or alcohol. Again I scored this so called 'negative index' with 4, 2, and 0, according to 'yes, 'perhaps' or 'no' answers.

Now my clients became really interested. They saw how their frustrations directly led to pain. I began to wonder how this pattern might be changed. But at that point, some vital areas of human life, - i.e. how far they felt they had achieved their ambition in life, how hopeful they were for the future, whether their lives had any meaning etc., - were as yet missing from the questionnaire or Scale. At this stage five such philosophical questions were asked and scored from 0 to 20 each along a sliding scale, using a ladder for graphic illustration. So now I had 55 questions in all. With my improved interviewing techniques, the journey towards self-discovery could proceed at a much faster rate than before. By now I also had a more sophisticated mathematical computation at hand to enable us to arrive at accurate diagnosis and, later on, prognosis as well. The Scale has been validated over a long period of time and is taught to the helping professions all over the globe. It is used in hospitals for screening purposed, alongside other instruments.

As I pursued my work in such 'community care' setting, using my Scale as an aid in diagnosis and interviewing, to my surprise I began to learn that my previously perceived role as a helper was often either not appreciated by, or not particularly helpful to, my clients. The Scale helped them to sort themselves out, often without my interference; many began to move towards some action in order to change their situation.

My role was beginning to be threefold: a facilitator who allowed them to see their lives in a more global way, a tester who helped them check out the correct action that would follow from their own conclusions and a resource person with some knowledge as to how such action plans, whatever they be, might be realized.

At long last, I found that my real role lay outside the hospital or clinical setting, and that I ought to share this experience with others.

Ever since the World Health Organization appointed me as a Consultant in this field in 1964, I have been teaching this subject under the name of *Human Social Functioning*, a subject concerned with facilitating people's growth in the community, outside of a hospital setting.

Beyond discipline, structure and interviewing methods, Community Care has given me - and many colleagues now working with me – an opportunity to distil some principles of practice, theory and philosophy. None of these seem to me to be incompatible with clinical practices. But there are some basic differences in emphasis, as well as perhaps some new roads available now to Community Care.

I started by speaking about the increasing number of people who feel useless. I shall conclude by saying that we must update the skills of those who are practicing facilitating care in the community today. I see the *Caring Facilitator* as a very important part of our changing society. His (or hers) is a new role, primarily an educational role. A new generation of people, frightened of our changing age, needs to be assisted to find a firm footing in purposeful life. The medical profession and the caring facilitators must reexamine their respective roles, for their own benefit, as well as for the good of a newly emerging, dynamic society."

As I travel around the world and in your country too, my young German friend, I meet an increasing number of young people who can speak of practically nothing except their work. And if I listen carefully, they do not even enjoy their work – it is merely something to be done, a duty to perform. So as I listen during those interviews to you and to your generation, I say to myself: how easy it would be for a dictator of any color or creed to come along and speak to you once more about the world, or a dream, or a nightmare. You would not know the difference, just as your fathers did not know it. They too fell into the trap and gave up (or at least they thought they could give up) their individual misery and unhappiness for what turned out to be the greatest nightmare in human history, - the Holocaust.

You may turn to me and ask: "All right then, with what you have learned and with what you know, tell us, where should our way and hope lie?"

The answer is not easy. But I have endeavored to give you an answer in this letter. I told you how it is possible, in spite of what you are doing at this particular moment in time, to enrich your life and to find new meaning in it by discovering what you really can do and eventually must do.

I am not suggesting that you must necessarily change your job, or go into the streets to demonstrate for new, compassionate social order. I say that you have within yourself the power of creativity and healing, and this power needs to be found, understood, explored and expressed.

Keep in mind that you may not be able to accomplish these tasks all by yourself; - that you may need others – Therapeutae – to guide you and help you to grow. But as yet we do not have them around, so for the time being you may have to be your own healer and teacher, as I was my own too.

EPILOGUE II

"The Unconscious knows no time" …

I am sitting in Berlin-Dahlem, with my Social Work colleagues. It is the autumn of 1979 and we have today completed the Basic Course in *The Heimler Method of Human Social Functioning.*

The aroma of the Gold Block tobacco that our teacher, Prof. Heimler is smoking fills the air, while we, the participants of the course, are enjoying a glass of wine and some snacks. The atmosphere is relaxed and we are open to meet each other in a personal way.

Prof. Heimler tells us that he will have to undergo a gallbladder operation, and he is hoping to survive it and recover soon. Then, as every year in January, he shall go to his teaching post at the University of Calgary in Canada.

Someone in the group asks him: "John, nobody knows how long we will still be on this earth; do you have a *message* to give to us, us young Germans? Our generation of Germans needs your *message*! Can you write something for us about your life, your philosophy, your thoughts, your faith?"
Prof. Heimler, - whom we now call John – is relighting his pipe thoughtfully …

25th of January, 1980. Big snowflakes are dancing in the darkness and eventually rest on the big chestnut tree in front of the window of my apartment in Berlin-Charlottenburg. It is three o'clock in the morning. In a couple of hours I have to make a fire in the big *"Kachelofen"* (big tiled stove) and get ready to go to work at the Family Service of the Berlin Senate.

I have just finished typing on my small mechanical typewriter the third tape with *Messages,* which John has sent me. He had dictated his book on tapes while in Canada with his wife.

I feel completely overwhelmed.

Instead of being tired after those sleepless nights, transcribing *Messages*, I am filled with new energy and driven to go on until day light breaks through the darkness.

June 1981, Hendon, London. I am sitting in Prof. Heimler's office, translating *Messages* into German. I have many questions and John patiently answers them and explains.

November 26, 1990. I am sitting beside Prof. Heimler's hospital bed and discuss *Messages* with him, who has been my husband now for almost 6 years. We are making small corrections. So far no publisher has taken on the book.

"You know why they don't publish it?" Eugene Heimler asks. "Because it does not fit into any of their categories. People like boxes, and this book does not fit into any box."

But I have learned from him, the author, my teacher, my friend and husband, that we *Jews do not accept defeat....*
Never!
And so I decided: *"Messages must be published!"*

Eugene Heimler's *Messages* is a highly unusual book, which has enriched my life in remarkable ways. It has deepened my Jewish knowledge and identity and has been the spur to continuing Jewish learning. It was, no doubt, a contributing factor for my personal Jewish journey to *Am Yisrael*. It confirmed my early conviction that I belong to the Jewish nation.

My conscious path began in East Germany at the age of seven, when I wrote in my first notebook with the letters that I had already learned '*ISSAEL*'. (I had not learned the letter '*R*' yet.)

Thanks to the author who, at the time in Canada, had sent his *Messages* to me while I lived in West-Berlin, my path to *Israel* had become a reality.

I am writing these words in my home in Jerusalem, where I have been living for almost 20 years.

Today, the 4th of December, 2013, is the anniversary of the author's death. It was exactly 23 years ago to this day that Eugene Heimler left this world. Our memories of him and his legacy will be eternally alive.

I have edited *Messages* to make the book more readable. Therefore, I cut out repetitions and other parts of writings, to make it accessible to all readers.

I added an epilogue into which I placed the writings referring to the subject of work and to the author's method of *Human Social Functioning*. In the original manuscript these were placed in between chapters. I corrected grammar and exchanged expressions that the author used in his dictation on the tapes, for more fitting ones.

My cordial thanks go to my great helper, who wants to remain anonymous, for his advice and practical assistance while we were working on the book. He spent many hours of his precious time helping me edit *Messages*. His excitement, passion and commitment throughout the process were a great moral and practical support for me.

My warmest appreciation goes to my friend and well-known author Libi Astaire for her help in mentoring me through the winding road of the publication process. Her patience and encouragement were invaluable.

I want to express my sincere gratitude to the author's closest friend, Rabbi Dr. André Ungar, who, after I had transcribed the book from tapes in 1980, typed out the entire manuscript again, correcting the mistakes I had made, when I was not yet entirely confident with the English language.

My deepest, heartfelt gratitude to the author for his guidance and for passing on his knowledge, insights, and profound wisdom, is beyond words.

Miriam Bracha Heimler
Jerusalem, December 4th, 2013

Other publications by Eugene Heimler

Now available at Amazon.com

Night of the Mist

"A dramatic and readable book." — *The Times Literary Supplement*

"Behind the eerie, the manic, the disgusting, he still conveys the desirability of life, the variety of human behavior, the power of imagination. His own conclusions were not of hate, but of discriminating tolerance." — *Peter Vansittart in The Observer (London, England)*

"This book deserves a place of its own in the literature of Nazi horrors, as it deals with those events from an unusual aspect – the effect of them upon the victims themselves." — **Lord Russell of Liverpool**

"There is no self-pity in Heimler's writing; just wonder at man's inhumanity to man … the massage he brings is not one of horror but of hope; of a fight back to life, and a life well worth living." – *The Huddersfield Examiner*

"This book has an important lesson to teach – that faith in God and in the dignity of man can overcome the greater evils that men can devise." – *The Catholic Times*

When the Germans invaded Hungary in 1944, Eugene Heimler was twenty-one. His father, a socialist as well as a Jew, was arrested by the Gestapo and never seen again. Mr. Heimler and his new wife were taken from a Hungarian ghetto and deported in a cattle truck to Auschwitz. His wife and family died there, but he survived to be taken to Buchenwald and other camps in Germany. At the end of the European war, he escaped and found his way back to his native country.

NIGHT OF THE MIST is an account of a young man's experience under the Gestapo. It records the day-to-day events, the miserable conditions of existence, the physical suffering endured by the prisoners. But Eugene Heimler goes beyond a factual record of events. With a gifted insight he describes the deeper effects of suffering – on their minds. He writes not only of himself but of many others imprisoned with him: of the doctor and the architect, no longer middle-class gentlemen of authority, but near animals; of the girl, once gentle and intelligent, now offering her diseased body for a crust of bread; of the man who spent twelve years in prison for the murder of his wife, and who in the inferno of a concentration camp found meaning in life.

Yet, though he knew the worst of humanity, Heimler was able to regain his faith in God and in the dignity of man. He does not hate; and the horror of his experience is transcended by his compassion and deep understanding of spiritual values. The true message of this book is not one of horror, but of hope.

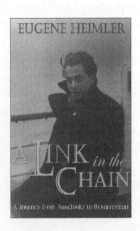

A Link in the Chain

This book is the story of life and resurrection

In this second powerfully written volume of Eugene Heimler's incredible life's journey from persecuted Jewish child in a small town in Hungary to world-renowned writer, therapist and teacher, Heimler is on his way home to Hungary from the concentration camps of Germany, where he had lost all his family. On this journey he experiences many life-threatening moments: being on a train with a former German SS man; witnessing the brutal rape of his traveling companion by Russian thugs; attempts on his life and being arrested and charged with treason in Hungary.

Eventually he reaches England and remarries, but his trials are manifold. After hearing that the Secret Police are torturing his friends in Budapest, he realizes he can never return to Hungary and has a breakdown. When a psycho-analysis helps him come back to life and regain his hope for the future, he is ready to act on an early ambition to become a writer and psychologist. He starts to write *NIGHT OF THE MIST,* which has become a world classic, and becomes a Psychiatric Social Worker. These challenges have their obstacles as well, and Heimler vividly describes his work as a Psychiatric Social Worker, including his refusal to give up on others — and himself. His experiences eventually lead to the development of a new method of therapy, which is today known as the *Heimler Method of Social Functioning.*

Throughout his life, Heimler consistently fought to help victims gain the courage to become victors. In *A LINK IN THE CHAIN* he once more tells his stories poetically and vividly.

For more information contact:
mheimler@bezeqint.net

6539601R00133

Printed in Great Britain
by Amazon.co.uk, Ltd.,
Marston Gate.